IMAGES
of America

BELFAST

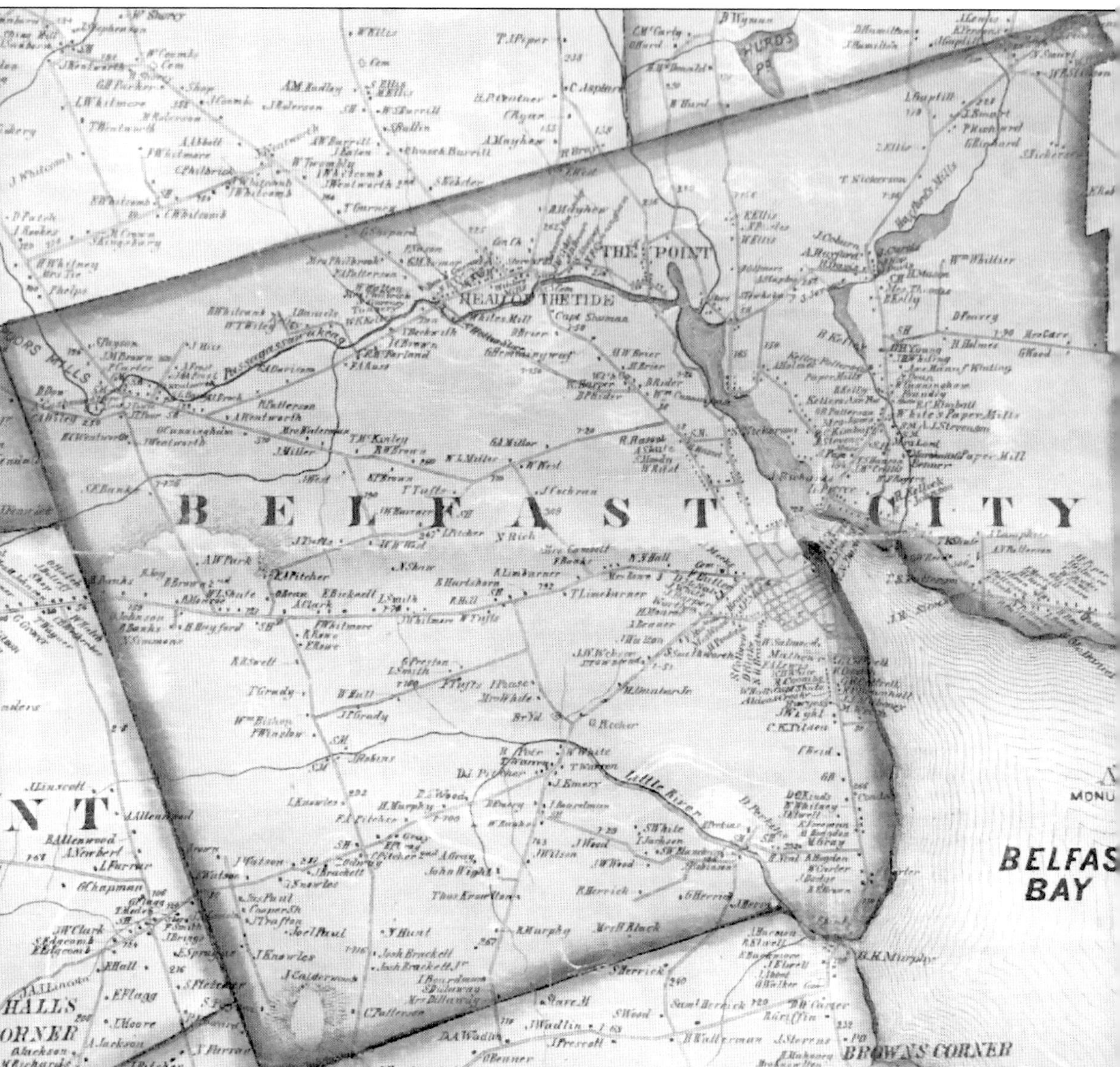

The coastal city of Belfast, Maine, is bordered by the towns of Belmont, Morrill, Northport, Searsport, Swanville, and Waldo. This detail is from the 1859 map of Waldo County published by J. Chace Jr. & Co. of Portland. These colorful and embellished maps contained business directories and engravings of prominent buildings. They were more important for establishing and promoting regional identities than for serving as navigational aids. (Courtesy of the Belfast Historical Society and Museum.)

On the Cover: With its proximity to shipping lanes in Penobscot Bay and the Atlantic seaboard, Belfast became the seat of Waldo County and its threshold to the world beyond. The bustling waterfront was crowded with wharves, warehouses, and shipbuilding yards. In 1870, investors established a railroad company to provide reliable transportation not dependent on winds and weather and to connect the city with the interior of the country. (Courtesy of the Belfast Historical Society and Museum.)

Megan S. Pinette and Jane B. McLean for
the Belfast Historical Society and Museum

Foreword by Earle G. Shettleworth Jr.

ISBN 978-1-4671-0453-1

Published by Arcadia Publishing
Charleston, South Carolina

Printed in the United States of America

Library of Congress Control Number: 2019949993

For all general information, please contact Arcadia Publishing:
Telephone 843-853-2070
Fax 843-853-0044
E-mail sales@arcadiapublishing.com
For customer service and orders:
Toll-Free 1-888-313-2665

Visit us on the Internet at www.arcadiapublishing.com

This book is dedicated to all the people who have kept Belfast's history alive by sharing their artifacts, photographs, and stories.

Contents

Foreword

In 2020, Maine's bicentennial year, the Belfast Historical Society and Museum is making a lasting contribution to the history of its city and state through the publication of *Belfast*. During the last three decades, Arcadia Publishing's Images of America series has produced many valuable pictorial histories of Maine towns and cities. Together, these books comprise the single greatest published archive of historical photographs of the state.

In this visual age, we want to learn about our past through photographs. A growing awareness of the importance of old photographs has led organizations such as the Belfast Historical Society and Museum to collect antique images to tell the story of their communities. Once given little attention, these pictures are now treasured sources of information.

As a prosperous 19th-century seaport and the seat of Waldo County, Belfast attracted photographers as early as 1841. Most Belfast photographers from the 1840s to the end of the Civil War made portraits of individuals and families. Beginning in the 1860s, the popularity of stereoviews as a domestic entertainment resulted in photographers expanding into outdoor photography. Between 1868 and 1890, four Belfast photographers made stereoviews depicting every aspect of the city. Today, their images constitute the most comprehensive record of the community's appearance in the 19th century.

Following passage of the Private Mailing Act of 1898, postcards grew rapidly in popularity as a convenient way of communicating, as souvenirs of travel, and as collectors' items. By 1900, postcards were replacing stereoviews. Given the economic vitality of early-20th-century Belfast, it is not surprising that the city served as the location for four major producers of genuine photograph postcards, documenting Belfast's appearance in the first half of the 20th century.

The rich selection of photographs found in this volume brings the past closer to its readers. As Lincoln Kirstein wrote of the 19th-century photographer, "His single task was to record the presence of every fact gathered within the net of rays focused on his lens, to create out of a fragmentary moment its own permanence."

—Earle G. Shettleworth Jr., Maine State Historian

ACKNOWLEDGMENTS

We are honored to present this volume in Arcadia Publishing's Images of America series. *Belfast* became a reality thanks to the help of the following: Belfast Historical Society and Museum Board of Directors, members, and volunteers who supported this venture; John K. Elberfeld, who scanned all the images and provided technical expertise; Larry Curtis, Liz Fitzsimmons, and David Ruberti, our beta readers who corrected and improved the book's content; Earle G. Shettleworth Jr., Maine state historian; Betsy Feeley, photograph archivist; Shirley Glubka, poet; Barbara Kramer, author of *Belfast and Searsport* for Arcadia Publishing; Belfast Free Library and Penobscot Marine Museum for access to their photographic collections; and our editors at Arcadia Publishing, Erin L. Vosgien and Caitrin Cunningham.

Unless otherwise noted, all images appear courtesy of the Belfast Historical Society and Museum.

Introduction

In her poem "October 12, 1865: Great Fire at Belfast Maine," Shirley Glubka writes of "the strange, living beauty at the heart of all fire." Her image could also be a metaphor for the heart of this city, which at first glance seems to be its striking architecture, welcoming waterfront, and unassuming lifestyle. However, Belfast possesses an energy, a "strange, living beauty," that draws people in and holds them here. *Belfast* is the story of the enterprising and resourceful people who have embraced this energy and, by birth or by choice, have made this city their home.

Belfast, the shire town of Waldo County, sits on the northwestern arm of Penobscot Bay, halfway up the coast of Maine. The Goose, Little, and Passagassawakeag Rivers course through the town and empty into the bay. For centuries, Penobscot people followed the patterns of game and fish as they hunted and gathered food in the area. The land and waters offered a bounty of beaver, otter, moose, bear, fish, seafood, birds, bird eggs, berries, nuts, and roots. In the summer months, the Penobscot erected temporary housing on the shores of the rivers and bay but did not create permanent settlements here.

By 1604, representatives of European business ventures were exploring the coast of present-day Maine and claiming land for the absentee shareholders. For the next two centuries, ownership of the land was in contention among the Wabanaki, British, French, and American peoples. Boundaries were established and moved during the French and Indian Wars, the Revolutionary War, and the War of 1812. Maine was part of the Commonwealth of Massachusetts until 1820, when it gained statehood.

In 1729, Boston businessman Samuel Waldo acquired controlling interest in a British land grant that became known as the Waldo Patent. The grant included parts of present-day Lincoln, Penobscot, and Waldo Counties as well as all of Knox County. In 1768, heirs of the Waldo family sought to sell some of their holdings. Thirty-five prosperous Scots-Irish farmers in Londonderry, New Hampshire, formed an association, or proprietary, for the purchase of 15,000 acres. A committee of three went to Boston to arrange the purchase for £1500, or about 20¢ per acre. A second committee arranged for a survey of the property from the Little River to Half-way Creek, in present-day Searsport.

The transfer of property was made in August 1769. The proprietors began planning for settlement and public improvements, including hiring a minister, clearing highways, and building mills. The first settlers arrived in the wilderness in May 1770, living in crude log cabins and clearing the land for farming. In 1773, the proprietors applied to the General Court in Boston for incorporation as a town. Their roots were in present-day Northern Ireland. The majority wanted to name their new town Londonderry, but James Miller proposed his hometown, Belfast. The story goes that the conflict was decided by tossing a penny, with Miller prevailing.

The first illustration on page 14 shows an artistic interpretation of Belfast in the late 1700s. The reader can almost smell the burning stumps and hear the scrape of the sledge being hauled by oxen. The 1843 lithograph opposite, on the top of page 15, shows a wide street with grand buildings, carriages, and a church steeple. What "strange, living beauty" drove the evolution of a backwoods wilderness into a prosperous market town and county seat in just 50 years?

The original proprietors may have been split in their choice of a name for their new venture but were single-minded in their purpose. They envisioned a town worthy of their families and progeny, a town with a school, a church, and commercial enterprises, all achievable through hard work and perseverance. They owned their properties outright and were not shackled by mortgages or indentures. They could afford to put their energies into development.

Geography played a critical role in Belfast's rise from what was described as a "horrid and uncultivated wilderness." The land around the town center was relatively flat. Camden, 18 miles to the south, had a deep harbor but was surrounded by mountains, making it difficult for farmers to reach it from the west. By using the rivers, people in the backcountry were able to travel to Belfast to trade their goods. The harbor provided access to shipping lanes in Penobscot Bay and thus to the Atlantic seaboard and beyond. By 1827, Belfast was the county seat of the newly created Waldo County.

The following section introduces the nine chapters of this book, tracing Belfast's history from the first proprietors through the centennial celebration in 1953.

Belfast developed quickly as a business center and market town for Waldo County. In the 1800s, one-third of its male workers were employed in maritime and related trades. The shipyards gave way to enterprises along the waterfront, including canneries, icehouses, grain mills, shoe factories, a window and door manufacturer, and poultry processing plants, establishing Belfast as a blue-collar industrial town.

The commercial buildings and stately homes of downtown reflect a time when Belfast was a flourishing seaport, shipbuilding center, and mercantile city. Over the years, the population has clustered downtown, at City Point, Upper Bridge, the east side, and Head of the Tide. Farms and small businesses have occupied the rural areas for well over two centuries.

Early settlers lived in log cabins in the wilderness. As Belfast grew to a prosperous market town, Cape Cod, Federal, and Greek Revival houses were favored over simpler dwellings. Wealthy businessmen built imposing homes in neighborhoods with attractive names like Primrose Hill. As prosperity continued in Belfast, older houses were refurbished to keep up with architectural trends, while new Victorian, Italianate, and Queen Anne houses appeared. The 20th century welcomed more modest manufactured and ranch-style houses.

Beginning with the original proprietors willing to risk their livelihoods in a new and uncertain venture, Belfast's citizens have shown themselves to be a forward-thinking group. Enterprising businessmen capitalized on the raw materials, ready labor market, and proximity to shipping routes to create a seaport and shipbuilding center. Local shipyards produced several hundred vessels, renowned for their speed, beauty, and excellent construction.

The incorporation of the Belfast & Moosehead Lake Railroad in 1870 provided a means of transportation not dependent on ocean winds and weather. Passengers, mail, and freight arrived and departed on fixed schedules. Steamships became a bridge to the 20th century, edging out the old schooners as they provided fast and reliable service up and down the coast.

Inspired by the mid-19th-century New England renaissance, Belfast citizens explored issues of temperance, spiritualism, scientific progress, and invention. In the 20th century, influential women enthusiastically joined their male counterparts in civic improvement, philanthropy, business, and public service.

The first local schoolhouse, a simple log structure, was built in 1794. As the population grew, so did the need for more schools, both centrally and in the rural districts. Along with educational instruction, students at neighborhood schools participated in activities and clubs, received health services, and displayed their accomplishments to their families. Young men and women were encouraged to go on to higher education, and many returned to practice their professions in their hometown.

For over two centuries, Belfast citizenry has been invested in the growth and welfare of the town. When Penobscot Bay was iced in, people hitched up their sleighs to take food and supplies across to stranded islanders. They turned out in numbers to assist during fires, snowstorms, floods, and ice storms. The illustration of the horrific fire of 1865, to which poet Shirley Glubka refers, is on page 95. Sometimes these catastrophic events resulted in improvements in municipal infrastructure, such as a fire hydrant system or stronger bridges.

Through the years, Belfast citizens have made their own fun. The town band played at outdoor concerts, and costumed "Horribles" entertained during Fourth of July parades. Miss Belfast and the Maine poultry queen were crowned at beauty pageants. Ship launchings were festive social affairs. Patriotic spirit ran high as downtown buildings were draped in bunting for Old Home Week celebrations.

The waterfront offered swimming, sailing, boating, fishing, clambakes, and chowder parties. People of all ages enjoyed winter sports, roller skating, and bowling as well as swimming in the saltwater pool at City Park. Civic and religious organizations provided sporting events, picnics, dances, outings, plays, and musical performances at the Opera House.

Since the late 19th century, vacationers have come to Belfast to savor the beautiful scenery, fresh salt air, and relaxed pace. Well-to-do rusticators sought simple country pleasures like hiking and fishing as a relief from their city lives. The railroad and steamboats soon brought tourists seeking more amenities, and guesthouses and hotels scrambled to provide up-to-date accommodations and excursions. Families who enjoyed the area built permanent vacation homes and cottages, often along the seashore or waterways, thus boosting Belfast's population with "summer people."

With the advent of the personal automobile came a more transient group of travelers who explored Maine's coastal route. Campgrounds, motor courts, service stations, roadside attractions, and eateries appeared on the Atlantic Highway to accommodate this new class of tourists. Organizations held festivals and events, not just for year-round citizens but with an eye to attracting summer visitors as well. The centennial of 1953 celebrated the granting of the city's charter in 1853 and drew 15,000 townspeople and visitors to witness its grand parade.

Beginning in the early 1800s, several histories of Belfast have been written, including two magna opera by Joseph Williamson Jr. In addition, since the turn of the 20th century, professional photographers have recorded local persons, buildings, and events. The authors have drawn on this wealth of documentation to create an illustrated volume that tells the story of Belfast from 1768 to the middle of the 1950s. The reader is invited to step back in time and explore the strange, living beauty that is the heart of Belfast.

One

Belfast Views

At the turn of the 20th century, Belfast's waterfront was bubbling with activity. Steamships arrived and departed daily, and a railroad spur ran down to its own wharf. Boatyards built vessels powered by sail, steam, gasoline, or muscle. Warehouses and factories lined the shore, and freshly caught seafood was for sale. This unusual view of the waterfront shows a ship launching as it appeared from the bay.

Capt. Albert W. Stevens was a premier aerial photographer during World War I. In November 1923, as he was flying to a reunion at the University of Maine in Orono, he asked the pilot to fly over his hometown. Stevens took a series of stunning photographs of Belfast, the first images of the city ever taken from the air. The Passagassawakeag River, bisecting the city, was spanned by the new Memorial Bridge. The crowded and grid-like downtown contrasted sharply with the rural east side. Although the first settlements were east of the river, the west side was soon favored for its more accessible harbor. In the background, the Goose River flowed through an almost ethereal wilderness as it made its way down to Penobscot Bay.

An essential task in the early days of Belfast was to develop a town out of the wilderness. Men felled trees and burned the stumps to create fields. Oxen drew logs to the wharves, which had been built to accommodate cargo ships from Boston. The tallest trees were destined to become masts, while most of the logs became cordwood. Illustrator Sam Manning drew this 20th-century artistic interpretation.

Squire James Nesmith was Belfast's first postmaster and owner of the town's first store, located at Little River. In 1799, he constructed this large, two-story building at Nesmith's Corner on Main and High Streets for his residence and store. The original Federal-style hip roof and chimneys were later replaced, and the building burned in 1854. Descendants of the early proprietors and settlers still live in the Belfast area.

VIEW OF HIGH STREET, BELFAST, MAINE.
FROM MAIN STREET.

At its incorporation in 1773, Belfast consisted of trails and log cabins in the wilderness. By 1843, it had developed into a busy market town with wide streets and sidewalks, as shown in this view of High Street from Main Street. James Emery, a jeweler, created this lithograph showing townspeople and business establishments, with the North Church spire and grand houses of Primrose Hill in the background.

Waldo County was created in 1827 with Belfast as its shire town, or county seat. The new courtroom within the town house soon proved inadequate for accommodating judicial offices. In 1853, a two-story brick courthouse costing $14,000 was built at the intersection of Church, High, and Market Streets. The court moved across Market Street in 2019 to the Waldo Judicial Center, a $14 million building.

First Church, shown around 1910, is considered one of Maine's finest examples of Federal architecture. Built in 1818, the church reflected the Federal style in its balance, symmetry, and plain surfaces. The bell by Paul Revere and Son of Boston was set in place in 1819 and was the first bell in town. Local clockmakers Timothy Chase and Phineas P. Quimby built the town clock, which was installed in 1836.

Belfast in 1860 was a lively seaport with a busy harbor, churches, factories, and houses. The steamship on the far left and the smokestacks confirmed the advance of the Industrial Age into mid-coast Maine. A photographer stood on the east side of the harbor. Beyond him, looking like a stone wall, was cordwood stacked and ready for transport, possibly to limekilns in nearby Rockland.

Wealthy businessmen lived in opulent houses on Primrose Hill and looked out over the busy waterfront with its shipyards, seagoing vessels, and factories. Their view also took in the working-class Puddle Dock district and the undeveloped east side across the harbor. This photograph, taken two years after the devastating fire of 1865, shows some of the reconstruction that was taking place.

By 1911, the dramatic absence of ship masts emphasized Belfast's evolution from a busy seaport to an industrial center. The railroad, whose depot is shown at far left, transported people and goods to the interior of Maine and thus to the rest of the country. Dominating the lower end of Main Street were the Sibley shoe factory, with its pointed tower, and other manufacturers and warehouses.

Unlike many coastal towns whose main thoroughfares are parallel to the waterfront, Belfast's Main Street is a steep hill that runs perpendicular to the shore. In 1878, prosperity dictated that the old buildings make way for grander edifices. A Gothic Revival structure, similar to the Masonic Temple farther down the street, would soon replace the building on the right advertising Howe's Scales.

Although shipbuilding and maritime enterprises were still important, by 1881 the center of business was shifting up Main Street toward Post Office Square. In the Victorian manner, financial success was often announced with shows of ostentation and excess. Belfast National Bank constructed the flatiron-shaped Gothic Revival building, shown at front right. It was the first building in Belfast designated solely for banking.

Neither horse nor wagon was in sight as Main Street welcomed automobile traffic in the thoroughly modern 1920s. The traffic "dummy" in the center directed vehicles through the challenging six-way intersection at Post Office Square. Telephone and telegraph wires filled the air, old buildings grew upward as stories were added, and the doorway of the old Belfast National Bank was bricked in.

In the 1940s, parking meters were installed on Main Street. The cupola of the Pythian Block, shown in the upper left center, was rebuilt as a spotting station during World War II. Volunteers staffed the seven-foot-square observatory, watching for enemy planes and U-boats. These citizen observers, working with the US Army Air Force, kept the station open 24 hours a day.

In the 19th century, a large commercial building or "block" had retail space on the ground floor, with offices or meeting halls on the upper levels. The 1866 Hayford Block was enlarged over the years to include the Belfast Opera House. This upstairs hall was the setting for many community events and on New Year's Eve 1888 was illuminated for the first time with electricity.

Belfast sent 858 men to the Civil War. Approximately 100 perished from wounds, disease, or imprisonment. In 1881, veterans formed the Thomas H. Marshall Post No. 42 of the Grand Army of the Republic (GAR). They collaborated with city government on a tribute to their fallen comrades. Built in 1890, Memorial Hall housed the GAR on the top floor, municipal offices on the main level, and the fire department below. (Courtesy of Belfast Free Library.)

In the early days, small public and private graveyards served the populace. As large sepulchers and monuments became popular, the town sought a suitable cemetery to accommodate them. In 1835, Grove Cemetery, named for the maple trees lining its walkways, was established. The old section near the ornamental iron fence contains the graves of two governors of Maine and the first two mayors of Belfast.

In his 1878 bequest for a free and public library, Paul Richard Hazeltine stipulated that it be a "handsome, substantial, fireproof building." Belfast Free Library was built of red granite with gray granite finishings. The library opened on May 1, 1888, with librarian Elizabeth Maltby Pond overseeing 2,000 volumes. Over the years, the library has continued to receive bequests for improvements and additions.

Postal service was initiated in 1795. As Belfast grew, post offices operated in village homes, stores, and hotels. In 1857, the federal government completed a permanent building at the intersection of Church, Franklin, Main, and Range (now Beaver) Streets. Belfast was port of entry for the western Penobscot Bay region. The customhouse operated in several locations before moving to the upper floor of the new post office.

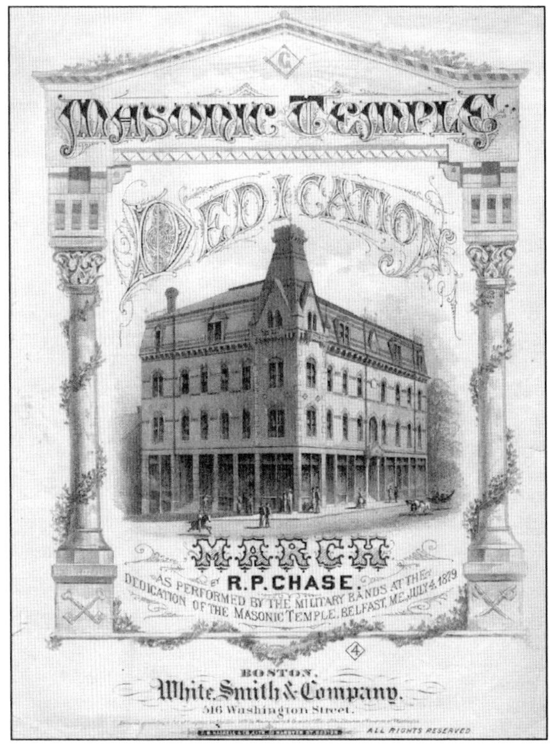

On July 4, 1879, the imposing new Masonic Temple on the corner of Main and High Streets was dedicated. This testament to Belfast's prosperity was built in Gothic Revival style and fitted with modern conveniences of water, gas, and steam. Ten thousand visitors arrived by carriage, train, or schooner to attend the festivities. Robert P. Chase composed this dedication march, which was played by nine military bands.

In the 19th and early 20th centuries, many town and city streets were graced with the American elm. The tall trees adapted well to urban conditions and produced leafy canopies, making them easy to walk or drive under. The canopies often formed living archways across the streets and provided cooling shade during hot summers. Most of Belfast's stately elms later succumbed to Dutch elm disease.

Puddle Dock was a small cove that provided dockage at high tide. The gritty neighborhood was home to working-class families, bootleggers, and small industries. After the cove was filled in, the city used the area for a dumping ground in the 1930s, as shown here. During World War II, the dump was cleaned up in a scrap metal drive. Front Street Shipyard now covers much of Puddle Dock.

At the turn of the 20th century, Belfast recognized the need for a modern medical facility. The Ladies Hospital Aid Society, the Waldo County Hospital Association, and the community worked together to purchase and equip the David Peirce home on Primrose Hill. Waldo County Hospital opened in 1904 and served generations of patients in the old wooden building, being replaced half a century later by Waldo County General Hospital.

Belfast's earliest bridge across the Passagassawakeag River was built here in 1801 at the Narrows. A local corporation owned the bridge and charged tolls for its use. Battered by ice, floods, and constant tides, the bridge was rebuilt several times and finally closed in the 1950s. At one time, Upper Bridge was an active community, with several wharves, mills, and a small shipbuilding enterprise.

Passagassawakeag is a Penobscot Nation word meaning "sturgeon—his place" or "the place for spearing sturgeon by torchlight." The 16-mile Passagassawakeag River runs from Brooks to Belfast's harbor. In 1806, the first bridge at this site connected the east and west sides of town. The wooden structure had a draw, allowing schooners to pass upstream to City Point. This 1907 view of Lower Bridge looks toward the sparsely developed east side.

In 1921, the old wooden Lower Bridge was replaced by the Waldo County Memorial Bridge. The $400,000 span was dedicated to the memory of servicemen who lost their lives in World War I. The modern concrete and granite structure was wide enough to accommodate automobiles that were traveling the coastal route. It had a swing mechanism that allowed barges and larger vessels upstream.

Approximately two miles up the Passagassawakeag River from downtown lies a point of land that was originally named for early settlers. The railroad came through the area in 1870, and the new mail stop was renamed City Point. The small village featured a school, a church, shops, a tannery, mills, and a brickmaking factory. The old cemetery is a silent witness to the families who lived there.

Head of the Tide was designated as the farthest point upstream where the Passagassawakeag River was affected by the tidal action of Penobscot Bay. The early settlers used the river for transportation and waterpower. A small community grew at Head of the Tide. By 1797, a sawmill was running there, and in the 1880s, Richard Gurney operated this water-powered sawmill and gristmill.

A stonemason and carpenter by trade, the Reverend William Vaughan joined his parishioners in building Trinity Reformed Church on the east side in 1907. Lacking an accessible harbor, the land east of the Passagassawakeag River developed slowly and was mainly agricultural. People settled along the shorefront and the Goose River. Dams on the river provided waterpower for small industries, including paper mills and an ax factory.

In the 19th century, after devastating fires downtown, insurance companies considered Belfast a risk because it lacked a hydrant system. To ensure an adequate supply of clean water for municipal, industrial, and domestic uses, the city began a waterworks system in 1887. A 175-foot dam on the Little River south of the city created a reservoir. The dam and brick pump house are still visible along US Route 1.

From the earliest days, farming has been part of Belfast life. People raised their own food and additional crops or goods for sale. Farmers formed Equity Grange No. 170 in 1876 to promote agriculture in their community. Growing a garden, keeping a cow, and raising a flock of hens became vitally important during the lean years of the Depression and the rationing of World Wars I and II.

For almost two centuries, an elevated sea marker has warned navigators about Steele's Ledge in the outer bay. In 1888, a large square granite monument replaced earlier unstable structures. In 1912, the monument was illuminated with an acetylene-fired beacon on a small steel tower and served as a lighthouse for decades. The stone monument and tower still stand sentry in western Penobscot Bay.

Two

Home Sweet Home

Through the changing faces of housing in Belfast, the constant has been "home." Whether grand or humble, each home has a story to tell. For centuries, families have gathered around the kitchen table, by the fireside, or in the backyard. Photography became increasingly available and affordable in the late 19th century, prompting this family to assemble by the porch to record a special occasion.

Robert Miller, son of original proprietor James Miller, built this center-chimney Cape Cod in 1792. The engraving shows the house standing alone, with no neighbors in sight, at what is now the busy intersection of Miller and High Streets. In 1886, the property was purchased for construction of the new library. The historic little house was moved to Bridge Street and later torn down.

James Nesmith settled in a small Cape Cod house on this point of land at the mouth of the Little River in 1796. He ran the first store in Belfast at this location, later moving his business to Main Street. Farmers brought their corn by boat to Nesmith's tidal-driven gristmill here. A much larger house now stands on the foundation of this old home.

Jerome Stephenson moved to Belfast at the end of the Revolutionary War and settled on the east side of the Passagassawakeag River. In 1800, he opened Black Horse Tavern in his home, as was the custom at that time. Travelers on the main coastal trail warmed themselves by the big fireplace as innkeeper Stephenson served them food and drink. The antique Cape Cod now overlooks busy US Route 1.

In Belfast's early days, Thomas Whittier's tavern was the scene of many celebrations and was considered "the best public house in Maine." As postmaster from 1810 to 1813, Whittier also maintained the post office in his home. The 1801 Federal building on Primrose Hill had an octagonal rooftop belvedere providing excellent views of the harbor. The entrance was updated with a Greek Revival portico.

William Crosby, one of the first lawyers in Belfast, lived in this 1802 Federal house. His son William G. Crosby, twice elected governor of the State of Maine, lived here until his death. The house was later annexed to the imposing Crosby Inn and partially destroyed by fire in 1896. Governor Crosby's granddaughter purchased and restored the family dwelling, which was later razed to create commercial space.

Bohan P. Field was a Dartmouth-educated lawyer who established Belfast's first law office in 1801. He was a respected leader in town affairs and was a commissioner for Waldo County after its establishment in 1827. His 1807 Federal house with its classic fanlight over the front entrance still sits on Primrose Hill. From the hilltop, Field had spectacular views down to the Passagassawakeag River and the bay.

Ralph Cross Johnson was an influential merchant and businessman in the first half of the 19th century. In 1853, he was elected almost unanimously as mayor of the newly chartered City of Belfast. He built a Federal mansion atop Primrose Hill in 1812, adding Greek Revival features two decades later. In the 20th century, the house was the summer home of Adm. William V. Pratt and his wife, Louise.

This brick Federal building with its striking rooftop balustrade stands at the corner of Church and Anderson Streets. Capt. Hutson Bishop, an early trader, built it in 1824. Hugh J. Anderson, merchant and governor of Maine in 1843, later lived here. The sign on the tree advertises the medical office of Dr. Orris Vickery, who occupied the house around the turn of the 20th century.

Charles Treadwell arrived in Belfast from Portsmouth, New Hampshire, in 1827 and married a granddaughter of one of the original proprietors. He built this brick house with its distinctive gable-end chimney roofline in 1832. The successful carriage maker caught gold fever in 1849 and endured many hardships during an overland trek to California with six other local men. Treadwell returned to Belfast and continued his carriage trade.

Joseph Williamson practiced law in Belfast from 1816 to 1854. In 1845, he built this Greek Revival home with a large two-story portico and Ionic columns. His son, attorney Joseph Williamson Jr., lived here with his family on High Street after his father's death. Williamson Jr. wrote two very detailed histories of Belfast, chronicling the town's growth from 1770 to 1902.

The Greek Revival movement, flourishing from 1820 to 1850, was widely popular in the young United States as a symbol of its hard-won democracy. Designed by architect Calvin Ryder and completed in 1842, the James Patterson White house is considered today among the finest examples of Greek Revival architecture in the state of Maine. White, a successful merchant, served as Belfast's mayor and state senator.

The James Patterson White house is in the National Register of Historic Places. Its latticed, eight-sided gazebo topped by a birdhouse and weather vane was a later addition following the lines of elaborate Victorian architecture. Stylish ladies took tea and enjoyed the gardens and grounds in the sheltering shade of this Moroccan-influenced structure.

Charles Bellows Hazeltine was a successful businessman and noted sportsman. In 1859, he built this imposing Italianate-Second Empire house on Primrose Hill. One of the first houses in Belfast to have indoor plumbing, it displayed French crystal windows, a grand mahogany staircase, and eight marble fireplaces. Hazeltine; his wife, Frances; their two daughters; and the family dog pause by the veranda.

The Carter house on High Street, with a single-story ell leading out to the large barn, was typical of its day in 1874. Aside from stabling the family's horse and carriage, the barn also contained tools, gardening implements, sports equipment, and bushel baskets full of items "too good to throw away." Today, collectors can still find old barns in Maine filled with treasures salvaged by generations of thrifty Yankees.

"Big house, little house, backhouse, barn" describes the connected farm buildings developed by New England farmers to make the outbuildings accessible year-round. The family lived in the big house, with the kitchen in the little house, or ell. The backhouse might contain a woodshed, workshop, tools, wagons, and a privy. The barn housed livestock and feed. Members of the Bowen family are shown outside their classic farmstead.

Prominent merchant and businessman Charles Prescott Hazeltine served on several boards and held governmental posts. In 1875, he and Benjamin F. Bickford built an icehouse at the east end of Lower Bridge and shipped ice that was harvested from the Goose River. His 1874 Italianate home on Cedar Street showcased a third-story tower, second-story rooftop balustrade, narrow double front doors, and a projecting bay window.

Wholesale shoe manufacturer Oliver G. Critchett built this Second Empire house on High Street. The 1875 dwelling featured a mansard, or double-sloping roof, decorative window caps, porches, and bay windows. From 1911 to 1931, Dr. Eugene Tapley lived here and maintained a private five-bed hospital on the third floor. Tapley is shown sitting in his sulky, while his nurses stand on the porch.

The rising middle class of the 19th century had leisure time and disposable income, commodities which were unimaginable to their pioneering forebearers. Against a background of striped wallpaper, this stylishly dressed Victorian family reads in the parlor. They are surrounded by hanging and potted plants, a large family Bible, framed needlepoint homilies, bric-a-brac on curio shelves, small tables draped in tablecloths, a pump organ, oil lamps, and photographs.

Edgar F. Hanson was a colorful and dominant figure in early 20th-century city politics. He built Colonia Villa in 1892 as a showplace on the city's southern entrance along Northport Avenue. Hanson spared no expense on his opulent mansion and its turrets, porches, gingerbread millwork, bowed windows, stables, and formal gardens. The villa, with a sweeping view over City Park to the bay, burned in 1923.

Two-family, or double tenement, houses provided a convenient way for extended families to live near each other. Owners frequently lived in one half and rented out the second tenement. In 1896, Dr. John Chellis Ham and Alvin T. Condon built this Queen Anne Victorian on Northport Avenue. Music educators Elbridge and Emma Pitcher purchased the house in 1906 and lived there with their daughter Gladys.

In the 1840s, Irish immigrants lived at Puddle Dock, a waterfront inlet and industrial site just north of Main Street. Working-class families continued to live in the low-rent section of town in modest dwellings like this small shingled home. The area was also home to bootlegging and other illegal enterprises. As seaport activities declined, Puddle Dock's small cove filled in and became the city's dump.

Today, real estate advertisements claim "water views" to entice people seeking a relaxing, restorative environment. Belfast's busy waterfront in the 19th century was anything but serene. It was filled with the sights, sounds, and smells of maritime and industrial enterprises. Workers lived in multiunit houses built close together near the harbor where they could walk to work each day. This row of houses stands on lower Miller Street.

In 1890, the completed waterworks project required a sewer system. Planners claimed that the new system would discharge deep into the bay, with tidal action providing "harmless distribution." Laborers from Italy arrived in Bar Harbor and came to Belfast to work on the sewers, staying at what was humorously known as the "Bar Harbor House" in Puddle Dock. The building later housed a blacksmith shop and a garage in the lower section.

The Mile Tree on Northport Avenue marked one mile from a point near the James Patterson White house. The road was used as a trotting course and for timing the speed of horses. Retired businessman George Williamson built this 16-room "cottage" on 20 acres near the Mile Tree in 1901. He and his guests enjoyed the views across Penobscot Bay to Islesboro, Castine, and Blue Hill.

Anne Crosby was a generous benefactor of many city projects in the first half of the 20th century, spearheading the drive for the new Crosby High School. In 1913, she built a stucco summer home near the waterfront on Northport Avenue south of the city. Her "cottage" had central heating, electricity, plumbing, and eight telephones. The house stands today as part of a condominium complex.

People in small rural communities relied on their neighbors for help in times of need. They strengthened their ties with gatherings like this neighborhood picnic at Head of the Tide on a sunny day at the turn of the 20th century. Men and boys hauled out tables, chairs, and benches, while women and girls prepared special dishes and set the tables with china, cutlery, and flowers.

Three

Notable People

Entrepreneurial and influential men shaped the direction of Belfast's development for the first 125 years. By the 20th century, women were becoming a powerful force in the city's growth and prosperity. Espousing the spirit of equal rights, business owner and community activist Essie Carle was the first of 352 Belfast women to register to vote in September 1920.

Nathan Read, valedictorian of Harvard's class of 1781, invented machinery to adapt Watt's steam engine for boats and land carriages. Hearing of opportunities in coastal Maine, he left Massachusetts in 1807 and moved with his family to Belfast. Read, a former teacher, was an original trustee of the Belfast Academy, founded in 1808. A dignified and respected gentleman, Judge Read served as chief justice in Hancock County.

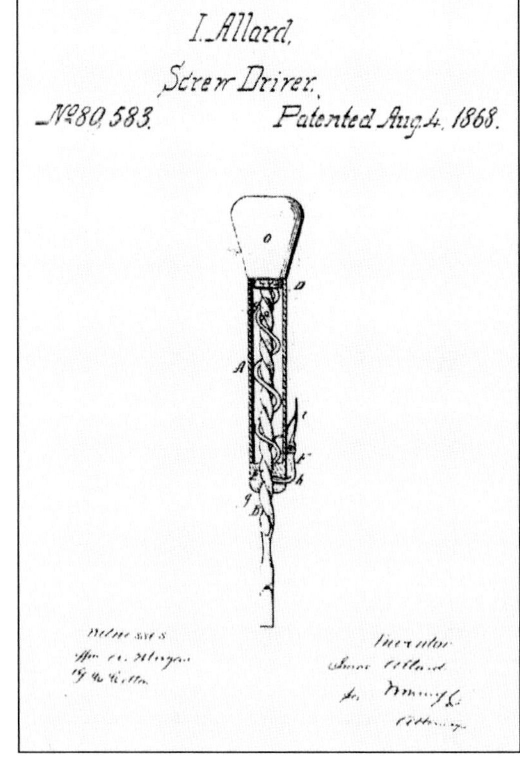

Many of the inventions patented in the last quarter of the 19th century were directly related to Belfast's industries, such as shipbuilding and shoe manufacturing. Isaac Allard Jr. was a watchmaker and machinist who received patents in 1868 and 1874 for the spiral screwdriver, a labor-saving tool that was operated by pushing down the handle. The Allard Spiral Screwdriver was produced by the Howard Manufacturing Company in Belfast.

Endowed with an inquisitive mind, Phineas Parkhurst Quimby apprenticed to a clockmaker at an early age. In 1836, he and Timothy Chase built the town clock located in the tower of First Church. Largely self-educated, Quimby was an inventor and philosopher. During the rise of spiritualism in 19th-century America, he claimed to have independent sight, or clairvoyance, and established himself as Dr. Quimby, healer of the sick.

In 1832, at age 19, Columbia P. Carter came to Belfast as a ship's carpenter. In 1841, he founded a shipbuilding enterprise that would continue with various partners over the next 35 years. Carter was a scrupulous businessman who believed in achievement through hard work. Using new and improved methods, C.P. Carter & Co. produced over 100 vessels known worldwide for their excellent quality.

During the Civil War, Belfast answered President Lincoln's call for help on the home front. Arbella Johnson, president of USG Society of the Ladies Volunteer Aid Society, led young women from the society in sewing an elaborate American flag quilt. The handmade coverlet, completed in three weeks, hung in Armory Square Hospital in Washington, DC, as an inspiration to the wounded soldiers there.

Tufts graduate Philo Hersey joined the 26th Maine Infantry Regiment and was promoted to lieutenant colonel in 1862. The following year he received a severe wound in Louisiana and was discharged. Hersey returned to Belfast, practiced law, and married Arbella Johnson. After the couple moved to California, he traveled by train to Belfast for reunions with his comrades at the Grand Army of the Republic post.

Joseph Williamson Jr. delighted in details and possessed a phenomenal memory for facts, incidents, and conversations. Born in Belfast in 1828, he graduated from Bowdoin College in 1849 and was admitted to the bar in 1852. An industrious solicitor and judge, he was also a prolific author. In 1877, he published the 900-page *History of Belfast, Volume 1*. The second volume was completed after his death in 1902.

Born in 1849, Percy A. Sanborn left school to apprentice with a local artist and engraver. He maintained a studio in Phoenix Row for half a century, painting people, cats, and horses as well as ships on commission for wealthy patrons. Most of Sanborn's oil and watercolor works were sold locally. He was also a violinist, composer, and poet. Shown is his 1870 painting of the Belfast-built ship *Ivanhoe*.

Born into a wealthy sea captain's family in 1866, Maud Gammans traveled extensively as an adult. On her return to Belfast, she was instrumental in raising funds to build St. Margaret's Episcopal Church, where local gentry and well-to-do summer people attended the Arts and Crafts–style chapel. Gammans's bequests to the city included an addition to the library, now the Gammans Reading Room.

Edgar F. Hanson was a dominant figure in Belfast politics in the early 1900s. An outspoken, energetic, and wealthy entrepreneur, he served 10 terms as mayor between 1895 and 1917. He challenged the city's political hierarchy and advocated for progressive initiatives such as a new centralized school. When challenged by the editor of conservative *Republican Journal,* Hanson founded and edited his own newspaper, the *Waldo County Herald*.

From a wealthy family who summered on Primrose Hill and wintered in Boston's Back Bay, Louise Johnson married William V. Pratt in 1902. They maintained a long-distance marriage during his distinguished naval career. A socialite with an aristocratic bearing, the well-traveled Louise Pratt spent part of the year in Belfast. She served as the founding president of Belfast Suffrage League in 1916.

The son of a steamship captain, William Veazie Pratt was born into wealth in 1869. After graduating from the US Naval Academy, he advanced steadily to the rank of admiral. A disciplined and pragmatic officer, Admiral Pratt served in World Wars I and II. From 1930 to 1933, as chief of naval operations and deputy to the secretary of the Navy, he advised President Hoover on peacetime naval policies.

Emma Pitcher, vocalist and pianist, was dedicated to the pursuit of musical endeavors. She and her husband, Elbridge, produced musical theatrical programs locally. They brought music education into the schools, using innovative devices such as the phonograph and projected slides. Emma Pitcher was instrumental in introducing formalized music study to public schools in Maine and became a state supervisor in that field.

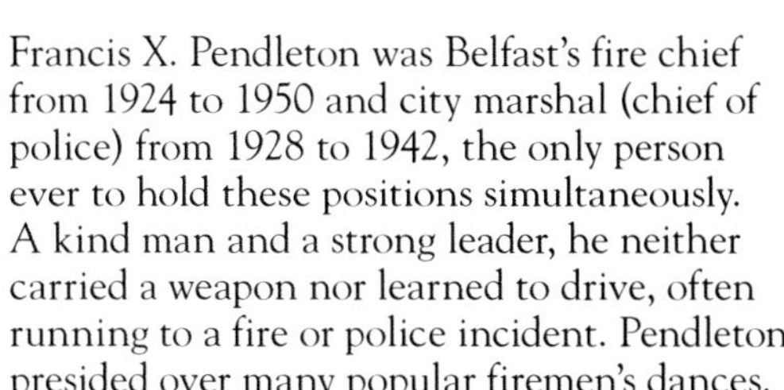

Francis X. Pendleton was Belfast's fire chief from 1924 to 1950 and city marshal (chief of police) from 1928 to 1942, the only person ever to hold these positions simultaneously. A kind man and a strong leader, he neither carried a weapon nor learned to drive, often running to a fire or police incident. Pendleton presided over many popular firemen's dances.

Anne Crosby Johnson, granddaughter of former governor William G. Crosby, generously contributed to many municipal projects throughout the city. She was a driving force behind the construction of the new high school, named for her grandfather and dedicated in 1924. Johnson donated the stone gateway to City Park, supported Waldo County Hospital, was a benefactor of the Belfast Youth Center, and contributed to St. Margaret's Episcopal Church.

The old wooden Lower Bridge was not built to withstand automobile traffic. In 1920, Hodgdon C. Buzzell vigorously advocated for its replacement in the State House of Representatives, where he was the Republican floor leader. The Waldo County Memorial Bridge, also known as "Busy Buzzell's Belfast Bridge," was dedicated in 1921. He continued to ascend the political ladder, becoming president of the state senate in 1925 and mayor of Belfast in 1942.

The ratification of the Nineteenth Amendment in 1920 paved the way for women to vote and to hold public office. In 1928, Blanche D. Clay ran as a Republican candidate for state representative in Augusta. Her platform stood firmly on her involvement in civic welfare causes, including appointments as overseer of the poor and as public health officer. She lost the primary in a fairly close race.

In the first quarter of the 20th century, progress put a strain on Belfast's resources, and the mayor's office was heavily entwined with politics. In 1929, the city adopted a business management form of government to increase efficiency. Harrie Eckler, hired as city manager, took on ambitious Depression-era projects. These included reducing the city's sizeable debt, opening an unemployment office, and administering federal work programs.

From an early age, Albert William Stevens displayed an inventive and fearless nature. A captain in the Army Air Corps, he made innovations in the fledgling field of aerial photography. In 1935, he commanded the joint National Geographic-Army Air Corps Explorer II stratospheric ascent mission, rising to a record-breaking 13.71 miles. During this flight, Stevens, right, took the first photographs to show the curvature of the Earth.

Clyde B. Holmes acquired coal, wood, and hay companies, regrouping them as Consumers Fuel. As his small energy empire grew, he purchased two tugboats, moved them to Belfast, and formed Eastern Maine Towing in 1943. His tugboat company added a new chapter to Belfast's rich maritime heritage. "Commodore" Holmes was active in civic affairs and served on Waldo County General Hospital's building committee.

George Robertson was known as the "friend of boys." While running a printing business in the Hayford Block, he led many activities and organized a chapter of Boys Clubs of America. During the Depression, Robertson, standing far left, took groups hiking and camping in the mountains. In 1952, a new elementary school to accommodate the postwar baby boom was built and named the George H. Robertson School.

Elena Shute graduated from Crosby High School and New England Conservatory of Music. She was the first Maine woman to appear on experimental television, performing a comedy monologue on a Boston shortwave station in 1931. As a member of the organizing committee for Belfast's centennial celebration in 1953, she drew on her theatrical experience to plan festive events. Shute was appointed Belfast's first woman acting postmaster in 1951.

Four

SAIL, RAIL, AND STEAM

Belfast's proximity to shipping lanes in Penobscot Bay and the Atlantic seaboard secured its place as the seat of Waldo County and its threshold to the world beyond. Shipyards produced sailing vessels known worldwide for their workmanship. The railroad provided reliable transportation that was less affected by winds and weather. Steamships became a bridge to the 20th century when Belfast capitalized on the growing tourist trade.

In 1793, Robert and James Miller built the schooner *Jenny Miller,* the first of 657 vessels produced in Belfast. By the mid-1800s, the waterfront was lined with shipbuilding yards, wharves, warehouses, and factories. One-third of the local men were employed in the maritime trades. Builders are shown working on a hull in Pendleton's shipyard in 1908, with three other ships in for repairs.

Commercial steam and sailing vessels worked alongside each other in the harbor for a century. Many of Belfast's brigs, sloops, and schooners sailed the East Coast trade route, where they were subjected to storms, gales, fog, fires on board, running aground, and collisions. Shipwreck annals contained haunting passages such as "1841. In October, the fishing-schooner *Two Sons,* with a crew of nine men, sailed, and was never heard from."

Statistics from the US Engineering Department showed that 1,250 vessels passed through Belfast's harbor in 1887. They brought grain, flour, coal, lime, iron, nails, grindstones, and salt as well as 170,000 tons of merchandise. They carried out hay, granite, ice, shoes, potatoes, apples, eggs, and 1.2 million feet of doors, sash, and blinds. The warehouse directly on the waterfront stored fuel, wood, and hay.

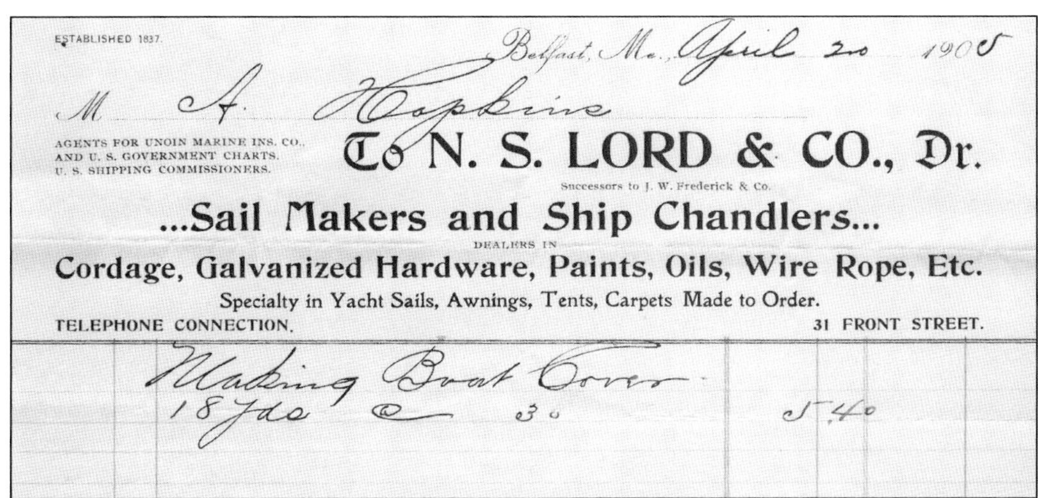

ESTABLISHED 1837.

Belfast, Me., April 20 1905

M A. Hopkins

AGENTS FOR UNOIN MARINE INS. CO., AND U. S. GOVERNMENT CHARTS. U. S. SHIPPING COMMISSIONERS.

To N. S. LORD & CO., Dr.

Successors to J. W. Frederick & Co.

...Sail Makers and Ship Chandlers...

DEALERS IN

Cordage, Galvanized Hardware, Paints, Oils, Wire Rope, Etc.

Specialty in Yacht Sails, Awnings, Tents, Carpets Made to Order.

TELEPHONE CONNECTION. 31 FRONT STREET.

Making Boat Cover		
18 yds @ .30		5.40

A ship's chandler, specializing in supplies for ships, was essential to the economic success of a seaport. Newton S. Lord operated a chandlery that had been established in 1837. The enterprise sold cordage, hardware, paints, and oils as well as yacht sails and awnings. In 1905, a new boat cover cost $5.40 for materials, no charge for labor.

With abundant lumber, steam-powered sawmills, and stretches of flat beach, Belfast became a shipbuilding center. Columbia P. Carter owned the largest shipyard, turning out 116 vessels known for their speed, beauty, and excellent construction. Ship launchings were popular social events where townspeople, owners, and workers gathered to cheer as the keel moved down the slipway and into the harbor.

Capt. Jeremiah O. Hayes made several voyages across the treacherous Atlantic during World War I as master of the Pendleton Brothers' schooner *Rachel W. Stevens.* In 1918, he set sail with a load of coal from Philadelphia, bound for Lisbon, Portugal. On his previous crossing, he had returned a month late after being thwarted by winds, which blew his ship hundreds of miles off course.

Freight rates and the cost of steel soared during World War I, generating a brief wooden shipbuilding boom in Belfast. Mathews Brothers built a vessel for Crowell & Thurlow of Boston, with Orlando Frost as supervisor of production. At 245 feet long, weighing 1,838 tons, the *Jennie Flood Kreger* was to be the largest and only five-masted ship ever produced in Belfast.

The March 1919 launch of the *Jennie Flood Kreger* symbolized the hope that Belfast would regain its prestige as a shipbuilding center and seaport. The launch party included notable people from New York City and Boston, who arrived by train. Capt. William Kreger, with hat and mustache, stood behind his wife, Jennie Kreger, far right, for whom the ship was named.

Eleven-year-old Katherine Frost, daughter of Mathews Brothers president Orlando Frost, had the thrill of her young lifetime when she attended the launching of the *Jennie Flood Kreger*. She reported the events of the day in her diary, noting the excitement of meeting the launch party and the creaking, grinding noise as the ship got underway. The steamer *Golden Rod* took everyone back to shore for a celebratory luncheon.

As the shipbuilding trade evolved from wood and sails to steel and steam, Belfast constructed only 10 sailing vessels after 1900. Fields S. Pendleton bought the Columbia P. Carter shipyard in 1899 and built a series of ships named for family members. His shipyard produced Belfast's last schooner, the four-masted *Blanche C. Pendleton*, in 1920. Her launch marked the end of a tradition lasting 125 years.

Recognizing the commercial importance of connecting with an established railroad line in Maine's interior, investors organized the Belfast & Moosehead Lake Railway Company in 1867. Although the western terminus changed from Moosehead Lake to Burnham Junction, the name was retained. The corporation lacked funds to equip and operate the enterprise and leased it to Maine Central Railroad in 1870.

In 1869, a local contractor advertised for 80,000 nine-foot railroad ties of cedar, hackmatack, yellow ash, or hemlock. The following spring two cargoes of iron arrived from England, and on June 4, workers began laying track. As the crowd cheered, Maud Milliken wielded the hammer to drive the first spike. By Christmas 1870, two trains were leaving Belfast each day.

The railroad yard was located in the Puddle Dock waterfront area, just north of Main Street. Despite very real concerns about the company's financial strength, ground breaking took place in August 1868. With great ceremony, the Excelsior Band and fire companies escorted the incorporators, city officials, and speakers to the depot grounds. Three young women, accompanied by cheering and music, used a miniature spade to turn the first shovelful of earth for this new venture. The Maine Central Railroad station is pictured above in 1904, as horse-drawn carts and wagons convey passengers and freight. The late-1930s photograph below shows the Belfast & Moosehead Lake Railway platform without its gingerbread trim. Today, the railroad in Belfast is marked by a multiuse rail trail; several miles of track; and a small, historic depot at City Point.

In 1926, following a 50-year lease by Maine Central Railroad, the City of Belfast began operating the Belfast & Moosehead Lake Railroad as the only publicly owned railway in the United States. Dignitaries and workers gathered in the train yard before joining the Fourth of July parade. Their float carried a scale-model freight car proudly displaying the "B&ML" logo and encouraging people to "Travel by Rail."

The Belfast & Moosehead Lake Railroad had no rolling stock and leased boxcars from Maine Central or Bangor & Aroostook Railroads. In 1940, the company acquired this 1901 steam engine, made in Manchester, New Hampshire. The old relic was sold for scrap in 1950. Railroad employee Charlie Hall recalled that in the winter, workers connected a steam engine to the station to heat the building.

NOT GOOD AFTER DATE PUNCHED			
Feb	Jan	1	DAY
Apr	Mar	3	2
Jun	May	5	4
Aug	Jul	7	6
Oct	Sep	9	8
Dec	Nov	11	10
NINETEEN HUNDRED AND		13	12
UNITS	TENS	15	14
0	0	17	16
1	1		
2	2	19	18
3	3	21	20
4	4	23	22
5	5	25	24
6	6		
7	7	27	26
8	8	29	28
9	9	31	30

AMOUNT COLLECTED

¢	¢	$
1	10	1
2	20	2
3	30	3
4	40	4
5	50	5
6	60	6
7	70	7
8	80	8
9	90	9

BELFAST AND MOOSEHEAD LAKE RAILROAD

ROUND TRIP CASH FARE RECEIPT

AUDITOR'S CHECK

No. 1165

GOOD IN COACHES ONLY

FROM

TO

AND RETURN

This portion is of NO VALUE except to Conductor, who must fill in spaces provided and forward to office of the Company as instructed.

W. L. BOWEN,
General Manager

ONE DAY RT ★
30 DAY RT ★
SPECIAL ★
TAX EXEMPT ★

If One-half ★ Punch Here

Form C. F. 4

In 1946, the railroad company replaced the steam engines with two General Electric diesel locomotives. The boxcars shipped out canned goods, shoes, and wood pulp and brought in chicken feed, coal, and gasoline. The poultry plant in Belfast transported processed chickens in a leased reefer (refrigerated boxcar). The train rolled along 33 miles of track, picking up a dairy car in Unity bound for the West Lynn, Massachusetts, creamery.

Walter Bowen took over as the down-to-earth general manager of the Belfast & Moosehead Lake Railroad in 1937. Trains transported passengers, mail, and freight between Belfast and Burnham Junction, where they connected with Maine Central Railroad. As more families acquired automobiles, Bowen had to contend with decreasing passenger numbers. After World War II, he watched a growing fleet of tractor trailers haul freight on improved highway systems.

Employees of the Belfast & Moosehead Lake Railroad produced the monthly *Waycar* magazine. It included reports from the managers, news items, jokes, and friendly rivalry among the station agents at Belfast, Brooks, Thorndike, Unity, and Burnham. Inbound and outbound freight traffic was reported. The November 1949 issue was dedicated to Waldo County chickens, noting that 185 carloads of poultry feed had arrived during October.

The Belfast & Moosehead Lake Railroad's

WAYCAR

Magazine

November 1949 Issue
Dedicated
To Waldo County Chickens

November 1949

In June 1950, the Belfast & Moosehead Lake Railroad made the final payment for two diesel locomotives. Company president Clarence A. Paul burned the mortgage papers in a ceremony at the rail yard, while a photographer from *Life* magazine recorded the event. The article never appeared in print as it was superseded by the news of the invasion of South Korea by North Korean troops.

In 1824, the first steamboat to come into Belfast harbor was the *Maine*, marking a new era in navigation. Steamers were soon providing rapid, reliable, and safe transportation for passengers and freight. Eastern Steamship Company of Boston, whose wharf is shown, had one of the most successful shipping lines on the Atlantic Coast before World War I. The company owned 20 ships, with routes covering 1,375 miles.

In 1882, the steamer *Penobscot* was built in East Boston for the Boston–Bangor line. She was the line's biggest and most sumptuous vessel to date and the first to have electric lights. The ship, shown arriving in Belfast harbor, was built from plans created by the company's officers and was considered to be difficult to maneuver and "a bad roller." The side-wheeler's saving grace was her beauty.

For over a century, steam vessels plied the waters of Penobscot Bay, carrying passengers, freight, and mail. In 1834, the steamship *Bangor* cut travel time between Bangor and Boston to a mere 36 hours, five meals included. At first, travelers at the Belfast docks scrambled over slippery rocks or were ferried in small boats to reach the steamers. By the 1850s, wharves in Belfast were extended to accommodate steam vessels and were widened to hold covered passenger and freight depots. The 1886 *Silver Star*, pictured above, and the 1893 *Golden Rod*, below, provided regular service to and from the coastal towns on Penobscot Bay. The coach for hire, or hack, at Lewis wharf was a dressy carriage with a driver out front and a pair of horses that clomped noisily over the wooden decking.

Winter ice forced the steamboats *Sedgwick* and *Castine* to be tied up at the railroad wharf. Co-owners and brothers Leighton and Perry Coombs operated the *Castine*. Their spotless and well-maintained vessel was very popular for Penobscot Bay excursions. In June 1935, with 75 Depression-weary passengers on board, she struck a ledge in dense fog, tearing a large hole in the starboard side. Four lives were lost in the incident.

Built at Bath Iron Works in Maine, the majestic steamship *Belfast* pulled into the Eastern Steamship Company dock for the first time in 1909. The 335-foot vessel was the largest and the last of the company's "great white fliers." She provided passenger and freight service between Penobscot Bay and Boston until December 1935. Overnight accommodations included an elegant dining room and 204 staterooms, with 222 more berths below deck.

Every flag, pennant, and bunting in Belfast festooned the Eastern Steamship Company's building as citizens joyfully welcomed the *Belfast* on her initial voyage from Bath. The massive 440-foot wharf at the foot of Commercial Street served the community from 1906 until the *Belfast* pulled away from her berth for the last time in 1935. The golden era of steamship travel in Penobscot Bay had ended.

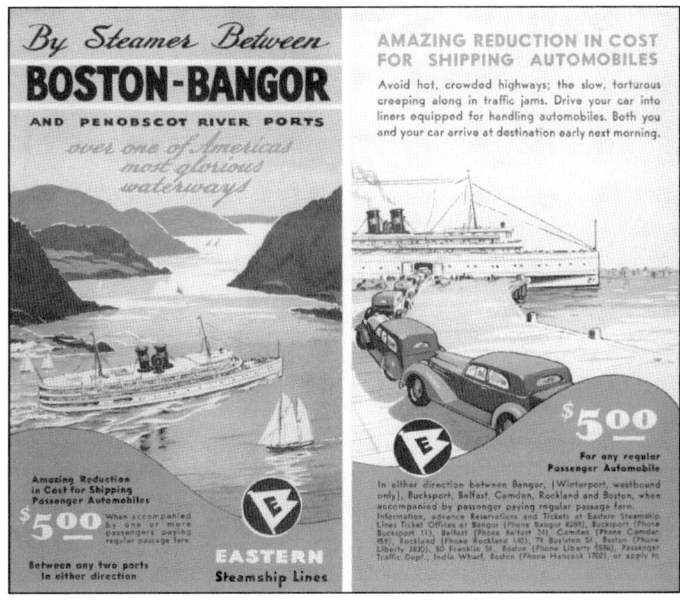

In the 1930s, Eastern Steamship Lines invited vacationers to avoid driving on crowded highways by traveling between Boston and Bangor on the SS *Belfast*. The westbound ship journeyed by river, bay, and ocean, leaving Penobscot ports in the evening and arriving in Boston the next morning. Belfast residents often commuted to Boston on the steamship for work or shopping expeditions.

Upon arrival, steamship passengers used the public telephone to make connections with their families or hotels. The sign opposite the Eastern Steamship Company wharf welcomed every craft coming into harbor. In 1915, the Board of Trade put up the billboard stating, "This is Belfast, The Biggest Little City in Maine." Although incorporated as a city in 1853, Belfast has never outgrown its small-town roots.

In 1936, Eastern Steamship Company's property was sold for lumber storage. Leo Luckey refurbished the wharf building in 1949 and opened a roller-skating rink and entertainment center, shown here. In the next decade, the structure collapsed into the harbor and was intentionally burned to prevent accidents. All that remains are pilings visible at low tide near the city's Boathouse at Steamboat Landing.

Five

SCHOOL DAYS

From the earliest days, Belfast has supported the education of youth. Following a state mandate that towns with 50 families or more provide a schoolmaster, citizens raised funds in 1794 to hire a teacher. As the population grew and spread on both sides of the river, so did the number of school districts. Shown are the handsomely attired Peirce School band members on the steps of their 1915 elementary building.

These brick buildings once stood on the Common at the corner of Church and Miller Streets. The schoolhouse on the left was built in 1827. The 1824 building on the right was originally a courthouse. It was converted to a high school in 1854 and later updated with a mansard roof. Both schools were razed in 1923 for the construction of Crosby High School.

Formal education for most 19th-century students ended at ninth grade. Secondary school instruction was generally reserved for the privileged few going on to college. The 1824 high school building was severely overcrowded, inadequately illuminated, and poorly ventilated. Despite the environmental challenges, faculty members were college graduates and provided a sound education. Belfast High School students advanced to Bowdoin, Colby, Cornell, Harvard, Radcliffe, and Wellesley colleges.

The 20th century brought a new era in learning, supplementing classical secondary school curricula with practical studies. The student population mushroomed, but the aging high school building was nearly condemned in 1907. The city was prohibited from borrowing money for a new facility due to the $500,000 debt incurred while building the Belfast & Moosehead Lake Railroad in 1870. Belfast High School was finally replaced in 1924.

Rural schools, like the White School on the east side, were often the center of community life. Families arrived by lantern light to attend Christmas programs. Students were on their best behavior at spelling bees and promotion ceremonies. In 1894, the city took control of its diverse school buildings and properties. One by one, the small schoolhouses were closed, and the city transported students to central schools.

In 1808, a group of men incorporated the Belfast Academy, a private school supported by subscription. Invading British troops were billeted in the academy's wooden building in 1814. That structure was replaced in 1846 with this brick Greek Revival schoolhouse on Church Street. Six years later, the academy trustees conveyed the building to the town, where it served as the South Primary School until 1915.

Soon after becoming a state in 1820, Maine required municipalities to educate their children. Belfast transported students to rural schools, first by horse and wagon and later by motorized vehicles. The central buildings were frequently overcrowded, with classes variously held off-site at Memorial (City) Hall, the Opera House, the old Coliseum, church rooms, and teachers' homes. Shown are lower grammar school students around 1900.

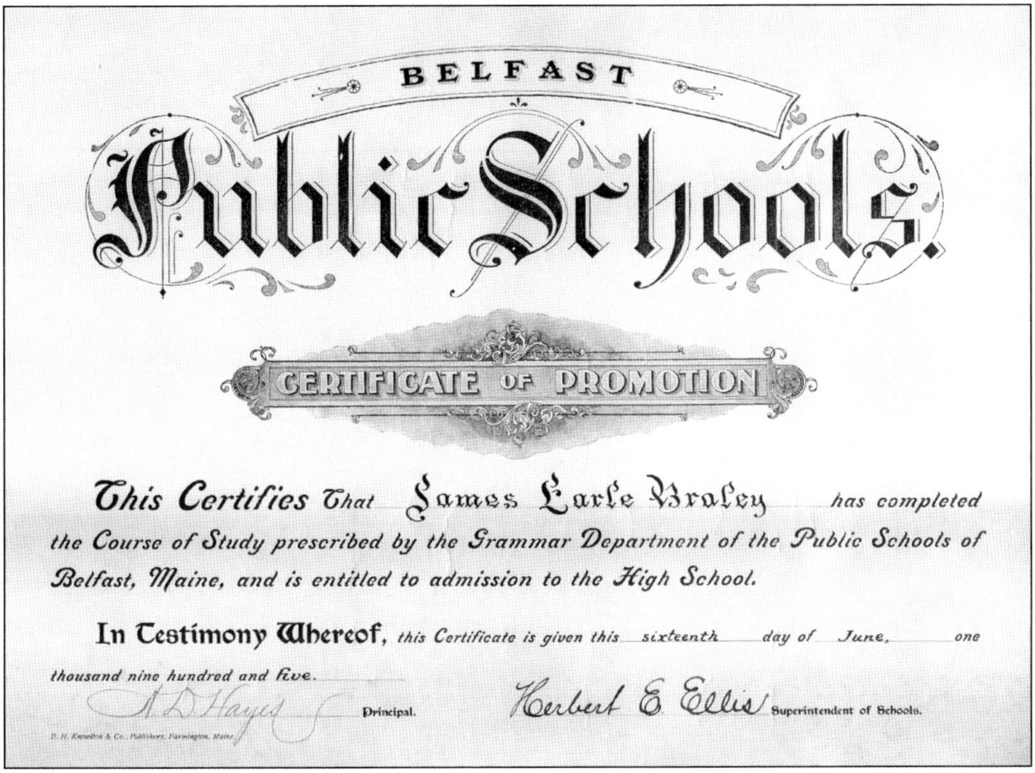

BELFAST

Public Schools.

CERTIFICATE OF PROMOTION

This Certifies That James Earle Braley has completed the Course of Study prescribed by the Grammar Department of the Public Schools of Belfast, Maine, and is entitled to admission to the High School.

In Testimony Whereof, this Certificate is given this sixteenth day of June, one thousand nine hundred and five.

A. D. Hayes Principal. Herbert E. Ellis Superintendent of Schools.

D. H. Knowlton & Co., Publishers, Farmington, Maine.

In 1904, Belfast High School made the New England Intercollegiate Examination Board's approved list, allowing graduates to attend almost any college in New England without an entrance examination. As the curriculum expanded to include required coursework, the high school changed from a three-year program to four years in 1916–1917. James Braley received this certificate promoting him to high school in June 1905.

When Clarabell Marsh graduated from Belfast High School in 1907, the young women wore white summery dresses and the young men wore new suits. The junior class decorated the stage at the Opera House with garden flowers. The salutatorian welcomed the guests, and the valedictorian closed with a farewell. The program included the class prophecy, musical numbers, presentation of the class gift, and awarding of the long-awaited diplomas.

In 1904, the first basketball game was held at the Opera House, where the high school principal and teachers coached the teams. When Crosby High School opened in 1924, physical education classes in the new gymnasium were added to the curriculum. In the lower grades, "physical education was obtained by a race down a hill," wrote a student of her days at Head of the Tide rural school.

These students became favorite storybook characters for a school production around 1915. National education reformer John Dewey proposed that students would thrive in environments where they interacted with the curriculum. This shift in philosophy required teachers to have training in current methodology. In the early 1900s, Superintendent of Schools Herbert Ellis urged his uncertified primary school teachers to secure normal (teacher) school instruction and receive state credentials.

Despite extensive repairs in 1899, the South Primary School on Church and Elm Streets was inadequate for 20th-century education. The eight-room Peirce School, named for benefactor Emma Peirce Frederick and her family, replaced the old building. It opened in 1915 and served the community until 2004. Maud Townsend's first graders are shown seated in their modern classroom with electric lights and tall windows.

In 1914, the school district was in turmoil. The high school building had nearly been condemned, the Upper Grammar and South Primary Schools were deteriorating rapidly, and the North Primary School on Bridge Street burned. Monies earmarked for a new high school were funneled into the pressing need for elementary school buildings. Three public-spirited businessmen secured the ivy-covered McLellan house on High Street for a new six-room primary school.

In the depths of the Depression, President Roosevelt's New Deal programs brought prosperity and hope to Belfast. City manager Harrie Eckler received funding for several public projects, including a new elementary school in 1934–1935. Through the Emergency Relief Appropriation Act, local contractors and laborers cleared away the old McLellan School (right) and built the Gov. Hugh J. Anderson School. The total project cost Belfast taxpayers $40,000.

In the early 20th century, team sports like baseball and basketball became popular, although students had to be transported by wagon or boat for intercity games. Motorized vehicles made travel to other schools easier, and by 1920, the first football team was practicing on the grounds of the McLellan School. Public interest in games at Crosby High School spurred the *Republican Journal* to introduce a separate sports page in 1933.

The subject of much political wrangling and financial vacillation, the sorely needed high school was completed in 1924. Anne Crosby pledged $40,000 as a seed fund to finance the school, requesting that it be named for her late grandfather, Gov. William G. Crosby. At the dedication in June, Gov. Percival Baxter commended the citizens of Belfast for making this wise investment in their children and the community.

The heart of the new Crosby High School was its auditorium, with a balcony and seating for 800. The community turned out for plays, cultural events, and musical programs. Although Elbridge S. Pitcher had introduced choral instruction at the old Belfast High School, the music program expanded greatly in the new building. In the 1920s, the school band won several titles in Class B statewide competitions.

The senior class play was a tradition that lasted well into the 20th century. The final play by Belfast High School seniors was held at the Opera House in 1923. *Springtime* was set in Louisiana in 1815, and the actors wore beautiful period costumes for the wedding scene. The play was coauthored by Pulitzer Prize–winner Booth Tarkington, who spent many summers on the Maine coast.

Mother is a Freshman was a popular movie starring Loretta Young and Van Johnson. In the early 1950s, the thespians at Crosby High School produced the comedy about switched identities at the mythical Pointer College. The back of this rehearsal photograph states that two cast members had to be replaced at the last minute, one felled by measles and the other by an accident.

Six

Making a Living

For over two centuries, Belfast has been the center of commerce for Waldo County, and small businesses have been its backbone. Enterprising shopkeepers have provided everything people would need from cradle to grave. In the late 19th century, members of the growing middle class could afford to trade in grandmother's uncomfortable old rocker for a plush new walnut parlor chair, delivered by R.H. Coombs & Sons.

People have long been salting, smoking, drying, and canning food to preserve it. In the 19th century, refrigeration of fresh food became popular when large blocks of ice could be shipped by modern transportation. In 1875, Charles P. Hazeltine and Benjamin F. Bickford put up icehouses at the east end of Lower Bridge and soon were exporting tons of ice harvested from the Goose River.

The Chase family of watch and clock makers operated a shop at this Main Street location for a century. Hiram Chase (center) stands in front of the store, which was well known for its fine products and excellent workmanship. Founder Timothy Chase designed and helped build the town clock in the First Church steeple in 1836. Today, it is one of the oldest town clocks in the state of Maine.

The enormously lucrative 19th-century patent medicine industry catered to people who were reluctant to see a doctor and to Civil War veterans seeking relief from pain. The Dana Sarsaparilla Company bottled a very popular concoction and made outrageous claims about its effectiveness, packaging written testimonials with every bottle. It is likely that the alcohol-based medicine, rather than curing diseases of the liver, contributed to them.

In 1854, Spencer W. Mathews started manufacturing doors, window sashes, and blinds. He was later joined by his brothers Noah and Sanford. In 1899, the firm passed to family members Clara Mathews, Addie Mathews, and Maud Mathews, becoming Maine's largest business owned and operated by women. Over the years, Mathews Brothers has been a steady, progressive employer and is today considered America's oldest window manufacturer.

In the 19th century, granite became a popular construction material, and Maine reigned supreme in the granite industry. The Oak Hill Granite Quarry opened in 1875 and in 1894 was connected to Maine Central Railroad by a spur terminating at City Point. The Oak Hill product was a fine-grained, dark blue stone whose beautifully polished surfaces are still seen today on monuments and gravestones.

Thanks to its harbor and relatively flat topography, Belfast became a market town for the outlying areas. Farmers hauled in their goods to sell, then traded with the local merchants. On this winter day, firewood and hay were for sale at Custom House (Post Office) Square. The ox on the left was filling up for his 14-mile return trip to Lincolnville that afternoon.

When shoemakers in Massachusetts walked off the job, owners looked to Maine for workers willing to toil for low wages. Starting in 1875, the Critchett, Sibley Company made shoes for a Boston firm in this huge wooden factory on lower Main Street. For nearly a century, shoemaking dominated Belfast's economy as its largest employer, with up to 500 workers producing 3,600 pairs of shoes a day. Steamships and trains brought in supplies and shipped out finished products. During World War II, Daly Brothers received government contracts to produce shoes and boots. Belfast native Larry Curtis recalls that his parents walked over a mile along the railroad track from their home at Upper Bridge to get to the shoe shop. In the summer, they carried buckets of home-grown garden produce to sell to their fellow employees.

In 1770, before a house had been built in Belfast, John Mitchell constructed a sawmill on Westcott Stream using materials he had procured from Boston. For three-quarters of a century, lumber was second only to cordwood as the town's principal export. Shown here are the men at Fair Holmes's lumber mill near Mitchell's original location, taking a break from their noisy, dusty work.

Due to a lack of photographs, it might be easy to forget all the construction workers who have created the infrastructure of Belfast over the past 250 years. They were responsible for building homes, roads, bridges, wharves, waterworks, sewers, schools, parks, railways, and power systems. The Lower Bridge, subject to wear and tear by the elements and vehicles, received new wooden decking periodically, as shown here.

As the tourist industry boomed, postcards became popular and inexpensive souvenirs. In response to this trend, Rudolph Herman Cassens founded Eastern Illustrating and Publishing Company in 1909. His traveling salesmen photographed the countryside and took orders for postcards at local businesses. Women in the small factory on High Street developed and hand-lettered the glass-plate negatives, producing "genuine photograph" postcards. At its peak, the company produced one million cards annually. (Courtesy of Penobscot Marine Museum.)

Out of necessity, children frequently worked in the home, on the farm, or with the family's business. Harold Colson (boy in center) shined shoes at the Colson Brothers' stand. No stranger to footwear, he later joined the workforce at the shoe factory. During World War I, the employees there put in 60-hour weeks to keep up with the military orders for shoes and boots.

From Belfast's inception, business owners collaborated to promote it as a market town. In the early 1900s, they drew in shoppers from the islands and towns around Penobscot Bay for Christmas excursions, promising a great stock of holiday items at low prices. Patrons boarded the *Golden Rod* steamer, spent the day in Belfast, ate lunch, did their Christmas shopping, and were home in time for supper.

Saco Valley Canning Company, based in Portland, built a plant in 1910 to process locally grown produce. The cannery operated from late July until Thanksgiving, employing nearly 50 men and women. September was high season for corn, which farmers harvested and shucked, then transported to the factory. Working 15-hour days, employees removed the kernels, processed them into creamed corn, and canned the product for shipment by rail.

William T. Colburn opened a small store in downtown Belfast in 1832, selling shoes and other items for payment in cash, produce, lumber, or cordwood. Although the business has relocated twice, it has been owned by only two families for almost 200 years. Colburn Shoe Store continues to do business under the original name, earning the title "Oldest shoe store in America."

Katherine Wilder-Brier operated the Wild-Brier Gift and Tea Room, a genteel downtown shop that featured lunches, gifts, and up-to-date hats and frocks of the 1920s. She belonged to the Business and Professional Women's Club, the largest organization of women in the city. The members strove to become better businesswomen while advocating for community progress. They provided college scholarships for young women and contributed to the schoolchildren's milk fund.

The cigar business flourished for a time in Belfast. Maitland Smith raised tobacco at Pearl Brook Farm, claiming the soil was similar to that in Connecticut. The leaves were dried in the empty Duplex Roller Bushing building on the waterfront, then trucked to F.M. Bailey's to be rolled into cigars. These tobacco plants were 40 days old and would be ready for harvest in September.

Before the days of self-service markets, home delivery of groceries, meat, baked goods, ice, and dairy products was common. Ben Field operated a shop on Church Street for many years, cheerfully delivering groceries by truck during the warmer months and by horse-drawn sleigh in the winter. Belfast's first supermarket, the A&P, opened in 1948 on Main Street, threatening the small businesses that had served the community for decades.

Fearless steeplejacks have no place in today's world of health and safety regulations. Ever mindful of the wind, George Dunbar used a system of rope pulleys and ladders to scale roofs, church spires, and chimneys. In July 1920, he gilded the weather vane atop the Waldo County Courthouse. From his nearby photography studio, Melvin A. Cook captured the event and printed postcards of the man with nerves of steel.

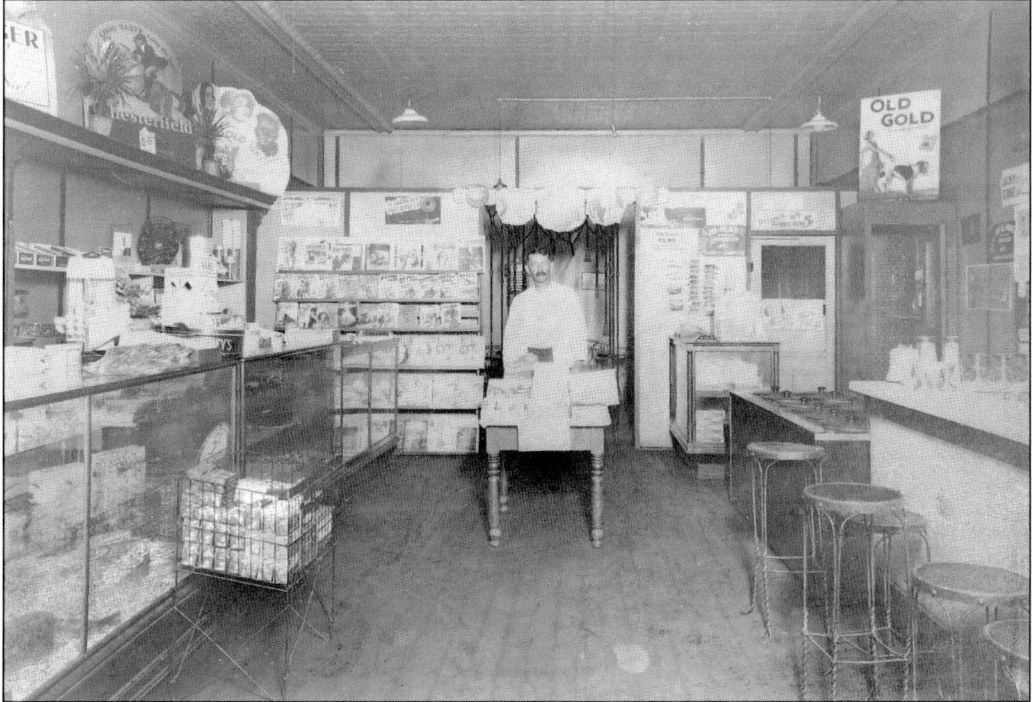

Father and son Fred and Everard Bailey ran the Belfast Candy Company in the Opera House. The shop sold a variety of nonessential items, including cigars, cigarettes, magazines, snacks, and, of course, candy. Customers ordered phosphate drinks and ice cream at the soda fountain and used the pay phone in the back. The candy store later became a favorite hangout for students from nearby Crosby High School.

The original proprietors of 1768 envisioned a well-organized and prosperous town guided by able leaders. For example, the quaint-sounding "culler of hoops and staves" was responsible for quality assurance of the barrels used in shipping. Over the years, the municipal workforce has grown steadily in administration, public safety, and maintenance. In the days before the environmental impact was understood, city workers dumped snow from the streets into the harbor.

In 1943, two barges were the first—and last—ships built in Belfast in 24 years. The US Maritime Commission ordered a small fleet of wooden vessels to transport equipment through mine-infested waters where steel-hulled ships could not go. The launching of the 194-foot barges was reminiscent of earlier times, with the Crosby High School band playing patriotic music and crowds cheering the *White Oak I* and *White Oak II*.

During World War II, five million women across the nation rolled their hair, rolled up their sleeves, and joined the workforce. Almost 400,000 women served in the military, while on the home front they worked in many jobs traditionally available only to men. In Belfast, women at Gunther Kleeburg's Maritime Quality Hardware Company assembled precision parts for military contracts, including these locks to be installed on warships.

Penobscot Bay fishermen caught immature herring and delivered them to local sardine canneries for processing. Employees at Belfast Packing Company worked tirelessly during World War II, with 55 percent of their output going overseas to the armed forces. In 1945, the Department of Agriculture awarded the company for outstanding performance in food processing. To commemorate the honor, the sardine packers and a well-fed cat gathered for a photograph.

Belfast Manufacturing Company, maker of men's and boys' pants, was founded in 1929. It was rated "essential" by the US government during World War II, meaning that an employee might be eligible for a short-term deferment from active duty. In 1944, the company completed a military contract for ski trousers and touted its patriotism by asking newspaper readers to "Imagine Uncle Sam with No Pants."

Following the industrial boom of World War II, Waldo County's postwar economic outlook was dim. Then a fortuitous combination of farmers with empty barns, a large and willing workforce, and the local railroad freight line catapulted Belfast into the poultry-processing business. Macleod Poultry Company started the first plant in 1945. With few environmental safeguards, the industry grew rapidly, and Belfast became the "Broiler Capital of Maine."

Seven

Newsworthy Events

In October 1865, a fire broke out and quickly spread through the tightly packed wooden houses, shipyards, businesses, and warehouses downtown. Efforts to control the blaze were hampered by strong winds, low tide, dry reservoirs, and insufficient firefighting apparatus. The "bailiwick of hell" consumed 125 buildings on 20 acres. Artist William M. Hall sketched the horrific scene, and his drawing was reproduced in *Harper's Weekly* on November 5, 1865.

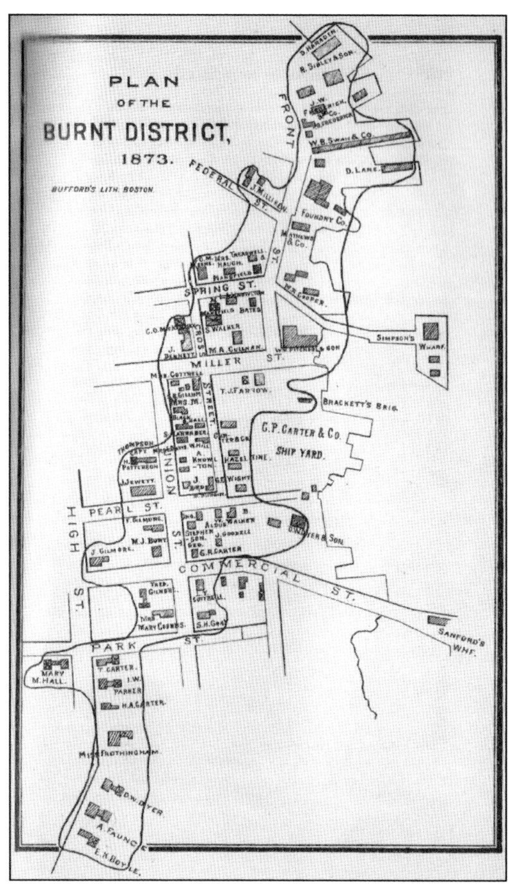

After the fire of 1865, the city passed an ordinance limiting the construction of wooden buildings in the downtown area. In August 1873, fierce winds quickly spread embers from a ship's cookstove along the waterfront and up the streets. The fire map shows the 20-acre area of destruction. Several new brick buildings were saved, but 75 working-class families were left homeless in "blackness and desolation of ashes."

Neighboring fire engines arrived by train or boat to assist Belfast firefighters during the 1873 fire. This dramatic view shows the boundary line of the inferno across the planking on Simpson's wharf, with cellar holes and chimneys in the foreground and untouched buildings beyond the fire line. After the city's second devastating blaze in eight years, Mayor W.C. Marshall appealed to the nation for financial assistance

Phoenix Row was an 1824 wooden building, or "block," of six stores on High Street. In June 1887, fire destroyed the old structure and threatened neighboring buildings. As a result, the Boston Insurance Exchange gave notice that insurance rates would be doubled unless Belfast procured a steam-powered fire engine. The city hired an engine for $50 a month, and the block was quickly rebuilt, this time with brick.

In January 1921, fire broke out at the foot of Main Street, destroying a large area that included the Pejepscot pulp yard and part of Consumers Fuel. January is generally the coldest month in Maine and a cruel time to fight a blaze. No matter what the challenge, Belfast's fire companies have bravely responded, from the earliest self-funded volunteer organization to the municipal department of today.

Early in the 20th century, audiences flocked to see moving pictures at the grand, 880-seat Colonial Theatre on High Street. In February 1923, a disastrous but spectacular fire after the last show destroyed the building. Manager Frank Petrich soon rented the Opera House and resumed showing movies. A new, modern Colonial Theatre was built on the original site, and 700 eager patrons attended opening night in January 1924.

Mindful of the threat by fire to lives and property, early citizens staffed bucket brigades and in 1821 raised money to purchase a Thayer hand-powered pump. Equipment, coupled with hydrants and a simple alarm system, improved over the years. In 1921, while horse team Tom and Jerry were still hauling an old engine, the city purchased its first self-propelled apparatus, a new American LaFrance.

In the early 1900s, the Waldo County sheriff handled most law enforcement cases. Francis X. Pendleton, first row center, became police chief in 1928. Under his strong leadership, the police department gradually assumed responsibility for peacekeeping in the city. In September 1933, the force handled a gruesome case involving a disgruntled man who shot and killed four people downtown, then took his own life.

The ice storm of January 1886 was unlike any in the memory of the oldest citizens. Branches bore up to 25 times their weight in ice, and the air was filled with cracking and crashing as limbs and whole trees came down. After the storm, sunlight created thousands of sparkling icy prisms. For several days, telegraph communication with the outside world was suspended, and all trains were delayed.

The winter of 1904–1905 saw thermometer readings plummet across the nation. Upper Penobscot Bay froze, and ice on Belfast harbor was 15 inches thick. When steamships and sailing vessels were unable to deliver fuel and supplies to the islands, townspeople sleighed across the bay carrying provisions. Horses pulling ice plows created a channel for US revenue cutter *Levi Woodbury*, which was pressed into service as an icebreaker.

The groundhog failed to predict the paralyzing nor'easter of February 1952. Thirty inches of snow and sleet fell, with fierce northeast winds forming drifts up to eight feet high. The storm brought all travel to a halt and forced snowbound residents to climb out their second-story windows. Before the drifts were cleared, High Street store owners dug tunnels to allow access to their businesses.

Belfast National Bank, chartered in 1857, occupied the Gothic flatiron building on Beaver and Main Streets. In 1909, the company constructed a new edifice across the street. Without emptying the massive concrete and steel vault, these workers maneuvered it through a hole in the wall, transported it across Main Street, and set it in the new basement.

In 1930, Texas Oil Company planned to demolish the century-old Treadwell house and construct a filling station on the corner of Miller and High Streets. In the interests of historic preservation, Louise H. Brewster purchased the charming brick house, had it lifted off its foundation and first floor, then moved it a mile down Northport Avenue. The move took several weeks, with a horse-powered winch inching the building along.

The United States declared war on Germany in April 1917. Waldo County men between the ages of 21 and 30 were conscripted. In September, the first recruits left for Fort Devens, Massachusetts, in a special train car. The Belfast Band, Boy Scouts, Civil War veterans, families, friends, and townspeople gathered at the depot to see them off. The crowd waved flags, hats, and handkerchiefs at this patriotic farewell.

The "war to end war" took place at home as well as on the battlefields of Europe. Families dealt stalwartly with shortages of food, fuel, paper, and clothing. Local businesses manufactured coats, trousers, shoes, and boots for the men "over there." On November 11, 1918, the armistice was signed, and the community rejoiced. Church and school bells rang, shop whistles blew, and schoolchildren cheered and waved flags.

In 1920, just days before construction of a new bridge was scheduled to begin, a truck went through the draw of the old wooden Lower Bridge. Driver and passenger jumped to safety, and townspeople turned out to view the vehicle stuck in the riverbed. The new concrete and granite structure with a paved roadway put Belfast on the Atlantic Highway, the coastal route that was beginning to attract tourists in automobiles.

On a cold day in October 1921, mounted officers led Company K and the Belfast Band as they marched down to the new bridge. Gov. Percival Baxter, in top hat, dedicated the Veterans Memorial Bridge to the men of Waldo County who died in the Great War. The span was replaced by a higher structure just upstream in the 1960s, and the old concrete pilings now support a pedestrian walkway.

America was poised to enter World War II in February 1941. Members of Company K, 103rd Infantry Regiment stood in somber formation at the Opera House before departure for training in Florida. Joining the US Army 43rd Infantry Division, they shipped out to New Zealand for the South Pacific campaign in October 1942. Sadly, the division's New England personnel were unprepared for the challenges of jungle warfare.

Landing ship tanks (LST) supported amphibious operations by delivering tanks, vehicles, cargo, and troops directly onto shore. The LST-512 removed German POWs from Normandy in June 1944. Subsequently damaged, she returned stateside for repairs and became a US Navy traveling exhibit ship. In July 1946, the LST-512 stopped in Belfast harbor. Nine thousand people toured the vessel, examined the displays, and talked with the crew.

Belfast soldiers, sailors, and pilots served around the globe during World War II. A large committee sought a fitting memorial to honor those who lost their lives in service. They chose the pool at City Park, rehabilitated it, and installed a bronze plaque containing 30 names. In July 1947, war hero Maj. Gen. Anthony McAuliffe helped dedicate the renovated pool, with 1,000 people at the ceremony.

By 1850, Belfast was on the rise, but the town system of government was inadequate to meet its growing administrative needs. Not without dissent, the town applied to the Maine Legislature for a city charter, which was approved by the governor. Belfast became the eighth city in Maine on March 21, 1853. One hundred years later, a three-day celebration to commemorate the centennial was announced.

COME TO

Belfast's Centennial Celebration

(ONE HUNDRED YEARS AS A CITY - 1853-1953)

August 14-15-16, 1953

FRIDAY - SATURDAY - SUNDAY

Parade - Field Day Events - Warship
Street Dancing - Band Concert
A Play, "Old Peabody Pew"
Special Church Services
Costume Ball
Featuring Baron Hugo and his famous band.

The 1953 centennial opened with Mayor Lewis Greene and city council members, in tall hats and satin waistcoats, reenacting the first reading of the charter. Events throughout the weekend included historical displays, a grand costume ball, sports and games at City Park, a street dance at Post Office Square, a horse show at the airport, and an alumni reunion with a member of the class of 1879 in attendance.

The highlight of the centennial celebration was the grand parade on Saturday. Fifteen thousand townspeople and visitors crowded the sidewalks to witness the mile-long procession. They cheered as 50 floats, five bands, baton twirlers, marchers, a miniature train, antique vehicles, and vintage fire apparatus went by. Members of the Business and Professional Women's Club wore heirloom clothing and decorated an old-time car with paper roses for their parade entry.

Eight

HAVING FUN

As early as 1849, the circus was a highly anticipated summer event. Advance men plastered the city with posters announcing "The circus is coming to town!" In August 1889, the show drew 10,000 people eager to see acrobats risking their lives and the menagerie of exotic animals. Arriving by train or steamship, the animals paraded up Main Street to the fairgrounds on Congress or Miller Streets.

A staple of New England Fourth of July parades was the Horribles. Their name was a play on "Honorables," and they satirized public officials and current events during patriotic celebrations. Clad in papier-mâché masks and grotesque costumes, the Belfast Horribles gathered on the post office steps in the late 1880s. Perhaps the birdcage suggested jail time for a politician or the broom called for a clean sweep.

Following the Civil War, baseball became the most popular American sport, and many communities fielded a team. In August 1872, the Boston Red Stocking Baseball Club played the Belfast Pastimes. During that game, the local scorer used nautical terms to note the lineup in his book: "Moody at bat, Boardman *on deck*, Dinsmore *in the hold*." Belfast made a contribution to the language of baseball but lost to Boston 35-1.

Bicycles took the country by storm in the 1880s. Robert Peirce opened a riding school at Peirce's Hall, where wheelmen could cycle on the second floor. The local men's Bicycle Club formed in 1888, and young women took up the sport several years later. George T. Read used these inexpensive advertising cards to promote his sales and repair business.

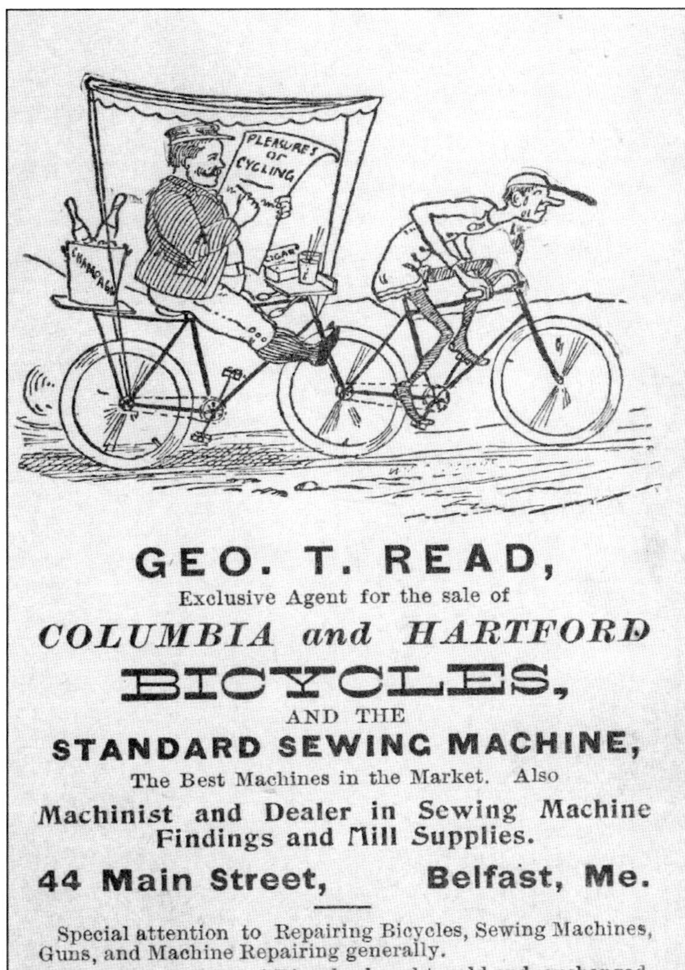

Belfast's shoreline is a fairly narrow cobble beach, which at low tide affords places for swimming, beachcombing, and picnics. Given the many hours required to produce an authentic New England clambake, it is likely that the food was prepared in kitchens and carried down to the water to be enjoyed there. This unidentified group brought bananas and liquid refreshment for its seaside outing.

Vessels in Belfast's harbor, from the earliest Penobscot dugout canoes to the great steamer *Belfast*, were generally working boats for fishing, commerce, and transportation. Toward the end of the 19th century, pleasure boating and sailing, no longer reserved for the well-to-do, became available to the growing middle class. One sunny day, this party sat at anchor in the power yacht *Isabel* near the Eastern Steamship Company's wharf.

Community theater is at its best when novices blend with seasoned performers, and Gilbert and Sullivan's operettas are perfect vehicles for this synthesis. The Colonial Theatre was the setting for this production of H.M.S. *Pinafore* in March 1917. Members of the Musical Society, joined by 50 students from Belfast High School, stood ready to declare, "For he is an Englishman."

The Belfast Band formed in 1889 and by 1900 was considered one of the best municipal ensembles in the state. The group was in demand for open-air concerts, parades, boat launchings, and political rallies. In the 1920s, the members assembled on the post office steps with Donald O. Robbins (left front), Belfast's well-known "man about town," and their leader, James Lee Patterson (right front, holding baton).

The 1920s have been called the first truly modern decade. People rebelled against the grim realities of the Great War. Prohibition was openly defied, and a new kind of music became standard in the Jazz Age. In Belfast, this jazz orchestra entertained at dances, parties, and social events. The musicians, with dinner jackets and pomaded hair, played current dance numbers, novelty songs, and show tunes.

The Business and Professional Women's Club entered the male-dominated sphere of commerce in 1923. While the members were invested in many civic improvement projects, they also found time to have fun. In January 1926, they held a fancy dress party, with half the merrymakers in male attire. Dinner was that delightful New England chafing dish favorite, shrimp wiggle, or shrimp and peas in cream sauce served over crackers.

Civic groups have volunteered countless hours for the betterment of Belfast since the firefighting bucket brigades of the early 1800s. Raising funds for their programs has been a constant endeavor, whether sponsoring theatrical entertainments, holding carnivals, or putting on harvest suppers. In October 1929, members of the Lions and Rotary Clubs staged an all-male "Womanless Wedding," and community leaders provided merriment with their female impersonations.

Beauty pageants and healthy baby contests, sponsored by local merchants and newspapers, were popular community entertainments in the early 20th century. Eileen Fernald, known for her poise and dancing ability, won the 1926 Miss Belfast contest. As victor of the beauty and popularity competition, she received a wristwatch and posed for an official portrait by local photographer Melvin A. Cook.

From 1870 through World War II, the Opera House hosted many community events, including high school graduations, choral programs, plays, boxing matches, lectures, and roller skating. In 1903, Belfast's first motion picture was shown there. Under a festoon of paper lanterns, the fashionably attired Ladies Hospital Aid Society held a tea to raise funds for Waldo County Hospital in 1927.

The five Jones brothers livened up summer days during the Depression with a backyard spectacle. They gathered friends to create the "Pigmy Circus," replete with a parade up Main Street to a field off Congress Street. Crowds adored their one-ring show, which included acrobats, clowns, hula dancers, dogs clipped to resemble lions, a fanciful flamingo, and a menagerie of family pets.

Levee and Ball

... BENEFIT ...

BELFAST FIREMEN

BELFAST OPERA HOUSE

Friday Evening - Jan. 30, 1942

— MUSIC BY —

GENE HAMMONS' ORCH.

OF BELFAST

January 1942 was a time of great uncertainty, as war had just been declared. The firemen maintained tradition with their annual receiving line and ball at the Opera House. Fire chief Francis X. Pendleton led the grand march, which was followed by waltzes, foxtrots, and quadrilles. Ice cream and cake were served at intermission. This souvenir card included a pencil for writing in the names of dance partners.

The Colonial Theatre, rebuilt after the 1923 fire, was renovated in 1947. Social events, beauty contests, and giveaway nights were gradually replaced by a cartoon and newsreel before the feature film. In 1947, moviegoers viewed the Elia Kazan film *Boomerang* with Dana Andrews and Jane Wyatt. The late show offered typical B movie fare, *Return of the Ape Man* starring Bela Lugosi.

Church members worked all year to get ready for their summertime bazaars. These events featured quilt raffles, games for children, white elephant treasures, handiwork sales, lunches, and sometimes strawberry shortcake. Since the earliest days, Belfast citizens have generously given their time and talents to governing boards, school committees, fire departments and auxiliaries, church societies, youth groups, and civic organizations.

Winters can be long in coastal Maine, with first frost usually in October and last frost often in May. Along with blizzards and ice storms come sunny days that are perfect for skating on ponds, rivers, and sometimes Penobscot Bay. Kirby Lake, also known as "The Muck," was a favorite place to skate, play hockey, or join a game of Crack the Whip.

Relatives traveled by boat, wagon, or car to attend the family reunion, that happy day of eating, catching up, and reminiscing. They arrived bearing baked beans, deviled eggs, cakes, and libations, legal or otherwise. The youngest baby squirmed in the lap of the oldest attendee, while teenage cousins giggled and gossiped. Often folks ended the day by harmonizing old tunes such as "In the Gloaming."

Nine

Summer People

Perry's Tropical Nut House billed itself as "the most interesting place on the Maine Coast" and remains a favorite tourist stop to this day. In 1926, Irving L. Perry started selling pecans and trinkets at his former cigar factory on the east side. Joshua Treat III took over the business in 1940, enlarged it, added curiosities, and sold gift items, including sweetgrass baskets handmade by Passamaquoddy and Penobscot natives.

Well-to-do rusticators came to Maine in the late 1800s seeking fresh air and simple pleasures as temporary relief from their urban lives. At first, they boarded with local families. Later, they were a boon to the economy as they began renting or building their own cottages, often along waterways. These vacationers at Riverside Cottage in nearby Searsmont enjoyed fishing and boating in Lake Quantabacook.

During the Civil War, two V-shaped defensive earthworks for artillery batteries were constructed on Penobscot Bay. The batteries never saw action and were dismantled in 1865. George Johnson acquired the property on the west side in 1889 and developed it as a private seasonal residential area. Townspeople and summer people built vacation homes on this land overlooking the bay. Today, the leafy, wooded location is still known as "The Battery."

In 1889, a group of investors built the Crosby Inn to attract more summer visitors to Belfast. It boasted 65 sleeping rooms, modern conveniences, and large balconies with commanding views of the bay. The inn, located on upper Main Street behind the post office, was destroyed by fire on a bitterly cold night in January 1896. The owners decided not to rebuild.

In the 1920s and 1930s, local residents welcomed the tourist trade by opening their homes to guests who were passing through or staying for a vacation. Postcards like this one provided inexpensive advertising and souvenirs. The Stickley-inspired Ivy House on Park Street was built in 1914, with furnishings designed by hostess Helen Shute. Artists, musicians, and opera singers often stayed at the shingled guest house.

Traditionally, hotels and inns were located near livery stables, coach lines, railroad depots, or harbor wharves. As vacationers took to the roads, accommodations followed them. Maine's motor routes were soon lined with diners, gas stations, roadside attractions, and tourist camps. The Thistle on Belfast's east side offered tidy private cabins with a view of the beautiful Penobscot Bay.

High Street's Colonial Inn and Windsor Hotel welcomed guests for over a century. In 1885, the State of Maine prohibited the manufacture and sale of alcohol. The largely unenforceable law was flouted openly in saloons and hotels until the statewide repeal of Prohibition in 1934. The following year, the Colonial Inn's billboard on the entrance to town enticed imbibers to visit Belfast's first cocktail room.

The Village Improvement Society, a group of influential women, spearheaded the movement to provide free public access to the shorefront. The city purchased 15 acres for $3,000 and created roads, gardens, and an arboretum. Belfast City Park opened to the public in September 1906. The pavilion provided a sheltered place to enjoy the beach, ocean breezes, and panoramic views of Penobscot Bay.

Belfast on Penobscot Bay
WELCOMES VISITORS
City Park - Free Camping Grounds
—BATHING—
Children's Supervised Play Grounds
Most Attractive Golf Course
within Two Miles

Distributed with
Compliments of
Business & Professional
Women's Club
Belfast, - Maine

America's love affair with the automobile began in the early 1900s. People embraced this new freedom to follow the open byways, often camping by the side of the road. Municipalities soon offered campgrounds as a way to curb littering by these travelers. Belfast welcomed visitors to City Park on the bay, promising free camping, swimming, children's activities, nearby golf links, and a business district just minutes away.

In the 1920s, the city began holding summer recreation programs at City Park, including swimming lessons at the beach. In 1936, a large pool was constructed through a federal work program. Filled with saltwater pumped in from the bay, the pool attracted thousands of families, vacationers, and community groups from near and far. Local residents still recall their swimming lessons in its bone-chilling water.

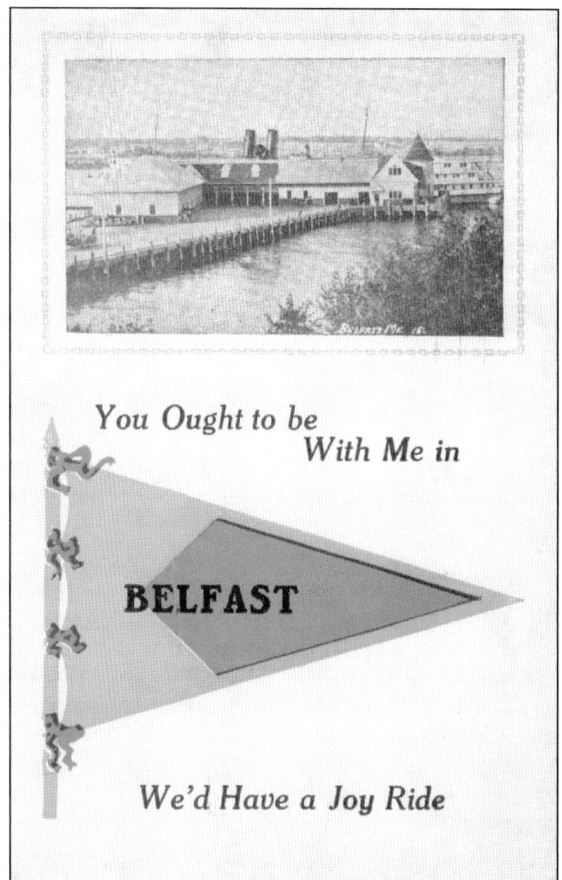

Almost as easily as electronic messages are sent today, visitors could keep in touch with family and friends by sending a postcard. At the turn of the 20th century, inexpensive picture postcards were extremely popular. Sometimes publishers would print a generic scene and insert the name of any town. However, this image of the Eastern Steamship Company's wharf shows that the card really is from Belfast.

Throughout Maine, the second full week in August was designated Old Home Week, a time for natives to return to their hometowns. In 1903, Belfast celebrated Old Home Week by commemorating the 50th anniversary of the granting of the city's charter. A Boston firm was hired to deck downtown buildings with flags and buntings. More than 200 homes and businesses were similarly decorated with stars and stripes.

Old Home Week celebrations included baseball games, church services, yacht races, receptions, reunions, band concerts, and musical performances. Local organizations participated in the grand parade of 1903. The women of National Boot and Shoe Workers Union Local 362 donned white dresses and liberty crowns to ride on their float. The local union organized soon after the shoe factory shut down in 1900, leaving 300 employees jobless.

The Waldo County Agricultural Society began holding fairs at its new grounds in 1860. The largest fair in the county featured a grandstand, half-mile trotting park, farm animal shows, and fancywork exhibits. As the agricultural foundation of the county diminished, the fairs were replaced by traveling carnivals. The grounds on Belmont Avenue were revitalized as a car raceway and later, in 1953, as a drive-in movie theater.

After World War II, a new industry boomed in Waldo County, the raising and processing of broiler chickens. Poultry farms sprang up throughout the countryside, and the fowl were processed in plants near the Belfast waterfront. In July 1948, the Maine Poultry Improvement Association, supported by the Maine Department of Agriculture, held its first Broiler Day barbecue at City Park. These women were enjoying the day's food, fun, and friendship.

While the poultry industry leaders were interested in crossbreeding a superior chicken, most attendees were more interested in tasting it. In 1951, ten thousand visitors flocked to the midsummer event in the "Broiler Capital of Maine." Eight tons of half broilers were delivered via refrigerated truck, dunked in special sauce, and cooked over two 100-foot barbecue pits. The meal included half a chicken, pickle, chips, and soda or milk.

In 1949, the Maine Poultry Improvement Association held the first Maine poultry queen contest in Belfast. Eighteen young women from around the state were judged on poise, personality, and appearance. While beauty pageant winners are traditionally photographed holding an armful of roses, the lovely Betty Perry, of Lincolnville, ruled the roost as she posed with a chicken at the 1949 Broiler Day festival. (Courtesy of Penobscot Marine Museum.)

Bibliography

Bunting, W.H., Kevin Johnson, and Earle G. Shettleworth Jr. *Maine on Glass*. Thomaston, ME: Tilbury House Publishers, 2016.

Davis, Jay, and Tim Hughes. *History of Belfast in the 20th Century*. Gaithersburg, MD: Signature Book Printing, Inc., 2002.

Dickson, Paul. *The Dickson Baseball Dictionary*. New York: Facts on File, 1989.

Early Histories of Belfast Maine. Rockland, ME: Picton Press, 1989.

Kramer, Barbara. *Belfast and Searsport*. Charleston, SC: Arcadia Publishing, 1997.

Williamson, Joseph. *History of the City of Belfast in the State of Maine, From its First Settlement in 1770 to 1875*. Portland, ME: Loring, Short and Harmon, 1877.

Williamson, Joseph. *History of the City of Belfast in the State of Maine Volume II 1875–1900*. Boston, MA: Houghton Mifflin Company, 1913.

About the Organization

The Belfast Historical Society and Museum is dedicated to the collection, conservation, preservation, and interpretation of documents, photographs, and other artifacts relevant to Belfast history. The society and museum, by means of museum exhibits, lectures, and other presentations, promotes the intellectual and cultural life of Belfast and informs and educates the Belfast community and visitors about its distinguished heritage.

In August 1953, Belfast, Maine, celebrated the 100th anniversary of receipt of its charter as a city. The occasion generated considerable interest in Belfast's heritage and resulted in the formation of the Belfast Historical Society in 1955. Twenty years later, on the eve of the nation's bicentennial celebrations, a brick Federal-style building at the corner of Market and Church Streets was purchased to serve as a repository and showcase for historic artifacts, memorabilia, and photographs. The Belfast Museum opened in 1975, and the two organizations incorporated in 1999.

The Belfast Historical Society and Museum maintains several outstanding programs that have received broad recognition. Museum exhibits and extensive archives provide educational and research opportunities for local students and other visitors. The organization sponsors Belfast's "Museum in the Streets," a walking tour of 30 permanently placed panels containing historical information. Two walking tour guidebooks of the residential and downtown historic districts provide information about the architecture of each structure and the history of the families who occupied them.

Off-site exhibits are maintained at the Belfast Free Library and the Captain Albert W. Stevens School. Programs of local historic interest are presented monthly at the library, and many are taped for airing on the local cable television station. Museum staff work closely with local schools, welcome student groups at the museum, and maintain a summer intern program providing training for two selected local students.

The Belfast Museum is located at 10 Market Street. For more information about museum news and the program schedule, visit www.belfastmuseum.org, call (207) 338-9229, or e-mail info@belfastmuseum.org.

MADE IN THE
USA